THE OLIVE TREE IN THE SHADOW OF THE SECOND TEMPLE

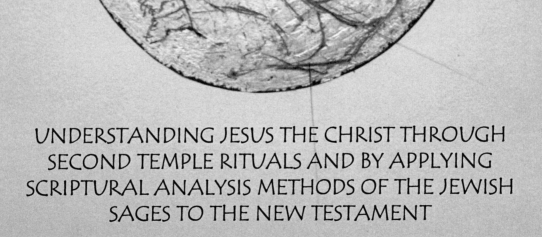

UNDERSTANDING JESUS THE CHRIST THROUGH
SECOND TEMPLE RITUALS AND BY APPLYING
SCRIPTURAL ANALYSIS METHODS OF THE JEWISH
SAGES TO THE NEW TESTAMENT

Commentary by Jeff Jinnett
Art and Illuminated Text by Sandra Bowden

DEDICATION

This book is dedicated to the Vatican's Pontifical Council for Promoting Christian Unity, Commission for Religious Relations With the Jews[1], which on December 10, 2015, issued the document:

> • "'The Gifts and the Calling of God are Irrevocable' (Rom 11:29): A Reflection on Theological Questions Pertaining to Catholic-Jewish Relations on the Occasion of the 50th Anniversary of 'Nostra Aetate' (No. 4)"[2] .

It also is dedicated to the Orthodox Rabbis who signed and published a responding document:

> • "Orthodox Rabbinic Statement on Christianity: To Do the Will of Our Father in Heaven - Toward a Partnership between Jews and Christians" (CJCUC: The Center for Jewish-Christian Understanding and Cooperation).

The preface to the new Vatican "Reflection" states that:

> "Fifty years ago, the declaration "Nostra Aetate" of the Second Vatican Council was promulgated. Its fourth article presents the relationship between the Catholic Church and the Jewish people in a new theological framework. The following reflections aim at … providing … a new stimulus for the future. Stressing once again the unique status of this relationship within the wider ambit of interreligious dialogue, theological questions are further discussed, such as the relevance of revelation, the relationship between the Old and the New Covenant, the relationship between the universality of salvation in Jesus Christ and the affirmation that the covenant of God with Israel has never been revoked…."

The Orthodox Rabbinic Statement on Christianity[3] states in response to the Vatican reflection that:

> "After nearly two millennia of mutual hostility and alienation, we Orthodox Rabbis who lead communities, institutions and seminaries in Israel, the United States and Europe recognize the historic opportunity now before us. We seek to do the will of our Father in Heaven by accepting the hand offered to us by our Christian brothers and sisters."

This book was inspired in part by the Vatican's 1965 "Nostra Aetate" Declaration and is intended to serve as an exploration through prose, commentary and art of the ecumenical principles and goals set forth in the above landmark documents.

---

[1] http://www.vatican.va/roman_curia/pontifical_councils/chrstuni/sub-index/index_relations-jews.htm
[2] http://www.vatican.va/roman_curia/pontifical_councils/chrstuni/relations-jews-docs/rc_pc_chrstuni_doc_20151210_ebraismo-nostra-aetate_en.html
[3] http://cjcuc.com/site/2015/12/03/orthodox-rabbinic-statement-on-christianity/

INDEX

Cover Artwork: "The Holy Family, after Michelangelo" by Sandra Bowden

Sometimes known as the Doni Madonna, Michelangelo's circular painting defies exact interpretation. However, certain elements suggest that Mary and Joseph appear to be presenting or giving the Christ Child. A prayer for Epiphany exhorts God to look down in mercy on the gifts of his Church, by which we offer "that which is signified, immolated and received by these gifts, Jesus Christ"; doni is the Italian for "gifts." Mixed media with gold leaf 2014 8" x 6" - Sandra Bowden

SELFSCAPE PRESS
San Francisco, California

Christianity as a Wild Olive Branch Grafted Onto the Olive Tree of Judaism

The Second Temple in Jerusalem was destroyed in 70 C.E., ending the era of Temple Judaism and giving birth to the era of Rabbinic Judaism and apostolic Christianity. Although the Temple and its rituals of animal sacrifices are long gone, the premise of this book is that an understanding of Temple Judaism, combined with later Rabbinic Judaism, can give Christians a better understanding as to the life and significance of Jesus. This book adopts the techniques developed by the Jewish sages in their scriptural analysis of the Torah and applies them to an analysis of the passages of the New Testament. Doing so hopefully will give the reader an understanding of Jesus that more fully fleshes out the concept in the Bible of Christianity being a branch grafted onto the olive tree of Judaism.

In Psalms 52:10, the Jewish people are described as an olive tree:

"But I am like a green olive tree
in the house of God;
I trust in the mercy of God
for ever and ever"

Rabbi Aha, a Jewish sage, also noted that Israel was likened to an olive tree in Jeremiah 11:16 ("A green olive tree, fair with goodly fruit")[1].

To the apostle Paul, Christians were like a wild olive branch grafted onto the olive tree of the Jewish people. As Paul wrote in his Letter to the Romans:

*"They are Israelites, and to them belong the sonship, the glory, the covenants, the giving of the law, the worship, and the promises; to them belong the patriarchs...[9:1-5] I ask, then, has God rejected his people? By no means! I myself am an Israelite, a descendant of Abraham, a member of the tribe of Benjamin. God has not rejected his people whom he foreknew...[11:1-2] If the dough offered as first fruits is holy, so is the whole lump; and if the root is holy, so are the branches. But if some of the branches were broken off, and **you, a wild olive shoot, were grafted in their place to share the richness of the olive tree**, do not boast over the branches. If you do boast, remember, it is not you that support the root, but the root that supports you... [11:16-18]... as regards election, they [Israel]*

are beloved for the sake of their forefathers. For the gifts of God and the call of God are irrevocable... [11:28-29] [emphasis added]"

This imagery of Jews and Christians being olive trees arises also in the New Testament book of Revelation, where both Judaism and Christianity act as witnesses to God at the end of the world:

*"And I will grant my two witnesses power to prophesy for one thousand two hundred and sixty days, clothed in sackcloth. These are the **two olive trees** and the two lampstands which stand before the Lord of the earth..."* Revelation 11:3-4 [emphasis added]

It is to be hoped that readers of this book will find my prose and commentary and the accompanying artwork and illuminated text of Sandra Bowden moving from a personal point of view. Hopefully, readers also will take away some sense of how closely related Judaism and Christianity are in faithfully standing witness to God's presence in the world and in the Holy Scriptures. At the heart of both Judaism and Christianity is a shared life-affirming world-view based on a spiritual sense of right and wrong - culminating in salvation in the world to come - which contrasts sharply to the nihilism so evident in today's postmodernist culture.

Just as Abraham welcomed travelers with food and drink in his tent and encouraged them to bless God for the food, it is hoped that readers of this book will be inspired to read the Holy Scriptures so that new souls will be awakened to God's glory. As Rabbi Joshua ben Levi said: "He who utters song [in praise of God] in this world will merit uttering it in the world to come, as is said, 'Happy are they that dwell in Thy house now; they will be praising Thee forever. Selah.' (Ps. 84:5)"[2].

It is my personal belief that only through immersion in both Jewish and Christian religious texts will a successful Jewish-Christian dialogue be possible. As Jonathan Swift, author of <u>Gulliver's Travels</u>, once said, "We have just enough religion to make us hate, but not enough to make us love one another."[3] For those who believe that it is inappropriate for Christians and Jews to read each other's religious texts, the Jewish Sage Rabbi Meir's words are noted:

"Where do we find proof that even a Gentile who pursues the study of Torah is like a high priest? From the assertion about Torah's ordinances that 'by pursuing their study man shall live' (Lev. 18:5), where Scripture speaks not of priest, Levite, or Israelite, but of 'man'. So you learn that even a Gentile who pursues the study of Torah is like a high priest."[4]

Organizational Structure of the Book

This book begins with "*Applying Scriptural Analysis Techniques used by the Jewish Sages to the New Testament*", which introduces three prose commentaries on scriptural passages from the Bible ("*Song of Ascents*", "*Sign of Jonah*" and "*Dominion*"). It is followed by an Epilogue which explains why the Jewish and Christian Holy Scriptures are "Trees of Life" for those who hold on to them – an antidote to the nihilistic, postmodern secular culture of the world. The Endnotes provide references to the primary and secondary sources underlying my commentary.

This books uses the analytical techniques developed by the Jewish Sages to interpret the Torah and other holy scriptures of Judaism, but applies them to the New Testament in order to better understand the significance of Jesus. The commentary includes passages from the Jewish holy scriptures (the **Torah** (the five books of Moses: Genesis, Exodus, Leviticus, Numbers and Deuteronomy), the **Neviim** (the writings of the Prophets: Joshua, Judges, I Samuel, II Samuel, I Kings, II Kings, Isaiah, Ezekiel, Hosea, Joel, Amos, Obadiah, Jonah, Micah, Nahum, Habakkuk, Zephaniah, Haggai, Zechariah and Malachi) and the **Ketuvim** (the Holy Writings: Psalms, Proverbs, Job, Song of Songs, Ruth, Lamentations, Ecclesiastes, Esther, Daniel, Ezra, Nehemiah, I Chronicles and II Chronicles). The Torah, the Neviim and the Ketuvim together are known as the **Tanakh**, which is an acronym formed from the names of the three sections. Two Masoretic texts of the *Tanakh* were relied upon for this book: (a) The Holy Scriptures: A Jewish Bible According to the Masoretic Text (Sinai Publishing 1996) ("Sinai Tanakh") and (b) The Jerusalem Bible according to the Masoretic Text (Koren Publishers 1997) ("Koren Tanakh").

It also should be recognized that when the Torah is referred to in Jewish writings, the author frequently is referring to the entire written and oral law, which would include the Tanakh (the written law) and the Talmud (the oral interpretation of the written law, originally passed down in oral form from generation to generation, but then reduced to writing). The **Talmud** is the compilation of Rabbinic law, comprising the *Mishnah* (literally, "second"; legal decisions contained in sixty tractates, organized into six orders and edited in the third century C.E.) and the *Gemara* (literally, "completion"; Rabbinic discussions of those laws, edited in the sixth century C.E.). The Talmud cited to herein is The Soncino Press 1989 Hebrew-English edition of the Babylonian Talmud, under the editorship of Rabbi Dr. I. Epstein. Whenever I refer to the "**Jewish Sages**" in this book, I am generally referring to (a) the **Tannaim** (the "teachers" or "repeaters" - first century B.C.E. to 200 C.E.) who transmitted the oral traditions which were codified as the Mishnah, (b) the **Amoraim** (the "interpreters"- third century C.E. through the fifth century C.E.) whose comments on the Mishnah are contained in the Gemara, or (c) medieval Rabbinic sages such as Rashi, Ramban and Bachya ben Asher of Saragossa.

In general, I have tended to use the Sephardi spellings for Hebrew words (e.g., *Shabbat*) rather than the Ashkenazi spellings (e.g., *Shabbos*), since it is believed that the Sephardi pronunciations are nearest to the original[5]. However, readers will find both Sephardi and Ashkenazi spellings for various Hebrew words in this book.

Passages from the **Christian Bible** (the Old Testament and the New Testament) also are included in some of the prose commentaries. All New Testament quotes cited herein are from the Revised Standard Version of the Bible (Thomas Nelson & Sons 1952) ("RSV Bible"). The Revised Standard Version is an authorized version of the American Standard Version, published in 1901, which was a revision of the King James Version, published in 1611, which itself was based on William Tyndale's English translation from the original Greek and Masoretic Hebrew texts.

Other related materials have been included, such as references to the **Dead Sea Scrolls**, which were written by a Jewish religious sect which lived in a wilderness settlement outside Jerusalem during the first century. The Qumran sect organized their religious calendar based on a solar calendar and appear to have supported the concept of Temple Judaism. They appear to have been opposed, however, to the Pharisees and the Sadducees, aristocratic Priests allied with the Roman authorities, who controlled the Second Temple in Jerusalem and who followed a lunar calendar. One commentator has theorized that sometime between 152 B.C.E. and 140 B.C.E., the Zadokites, the original Temple priests, were expelled by the Maccabees and that some of these Zadokite priests withdrew to form the Qumran community[6]. Another group of biblical scholars hypothesize that the Qumran community may have been zealots akin to the group at Masada, who also followed a solar calendar[7]. It also has been proposed that the Dead Sea Scrolls shows that Rabbinic Judaism and first century Christianity both evolved out of Temple Judaism - in essence as sister religions with a common mother religion[8]. Or as has been noted:

> *"For Jews, the Qumran texts say, 'Our family was larger than you knew'...For Christians, the texts say, 'You are more Jewish than you realized.'"*[9]

Finally, I have included passages from various ***Midrashic* sources**. A "midrash" is defined as a:

> *"Rabbinic story, parable or interpretation of biblical text, coming from the root d-r-sh,*

which means 'to examine'. These midrashim [plural of midrash] help fill in gaps in the text, supply missing details or dialogue, and enliven the text with personal anecdotes. Early midrashim can be found in the Talmud, from the second century, but the first actual compendia were edited in the fifth and sixth centuries C.E. Modern midrashim are still being written today."[10].

Another useful definition of a midrash is:

"any sort of homiletical material, often using symbolism, metaphor, analogy, poetry, alliteration, onomatopoeia, and other literary devices to express a thought, often related to the Bible, or based upon Biblical verses."[11].

In a way, the section of this book entitled "Song of Ascents" represents a "midrash" on various passages from the Tanakh, the Talmud and the New Testament.

Inspiration from Scripture

One of the underlying principles of this book is the inspirational power of scriptural passages. The following passage from the Dead Sea Scrolls describes the ultimate source of inspiration for this book, which combines prose and art in praise of God:

"You created breath for the tongue, and You know its words. You determined the fruit of the lips before they came about. You appoint words by a measuring line and the utterance of the breath of the lips by calculation. You bring forth the measuring lines in respect of their mysteries, and the utterance of spirits in accordance with their plan in order to make known Your glory..."

-Dead Sea Scrolls (First Cave of Qumran, Hodayot [Thanksgiving Psalms] Scroll, Column 9)[12]

As it is written in Psalm 22:4 [Koren Tanakh] - "But thou art holy, O thou that art enthroned upon the praises of Yisra'el" - *may Jews and Christians as God's two witnesses together form one Israel – one olive tree - and may their combined praises of God ascend to Heaven to form the very throne of God*[13].

Jeff Jinnett
San Francisco, California
December 13, 2015
1 Tevet, 5776

"Written"

This encaustic panel has beneath its layer of wax the text from Romans 1: "For since the creation of the world, God's invisible qualities—his eternal power and divine nature— have been clearly seen, being understood from what has been made, so that men are without excuse." Raised gilded panels echo Romans' intent and spirit with words from the Book of James, "It is written, the just shall live by faith." - Encaustic with mixed media 2008 20" x 16" - Sandra Bowden

APPLYING SCRIPTURAL ANALYSIS METHODS USED BY THE JEWISH SAGES TO THE NEW TESTAMENT

One of the central theses of this book is that Christians cannot truly understand and appreciate the religious significance of Jesus without an understanding of the surrounding context of Temple Judaism and of Rabbinic Judaism which grew out of Temple Judaism as a sister religion to Christianity. I firmly believe that Christians can gain a better understanding of the **Bible as Jesus knew it** by understanding how devout Jews may have interpreted the Bible in the first century C.E. For example, Christians are familiar with the Ten Commandments and probably think that they fully understand how Jesus would have explained the literal meaning of the Ten Commandments. And yet devout Jews in the time of Jesus may have interpreted the **Eighth Commandment** ("Thou shalt not steal") to mean that one should not **kidnap** another person. Under Mosaic Law, stealing material things was not a capital offense punishable by death, while kidnapping was. The Jewish Sages therefore reasoned that (a) since the commandment against stealing was placed just after the Sixth Commandment (prohibition against murder) and the Seventh Commandment (prohibition against committing adultery), both of which were capital offenses, and (b) just before the Ninth Commandment (prohibition against bearing false witness), which the Jewish Sages viewed as anathema to God[14], the "stealing" which was referred to in the Eighth Commandment therefore was kidnapping, the *stealing of a person*[15]. The stealing of material things would likely have been understood as being subsumed under the Tenth Commandment (prohibition against coveting possessions of your neighbor) or under Leviticus 19:13: "You shall not cheat your fellow and you shall not rob"[16].

I believe also that study of Jewish Torah commentary can not only enhance a Christian's appreciation of the plain meaning of a Biblical text, but also provide insight into the deeper symbolic or allegorical explanation of a text, and the sometimes hidden, mystical interpretation of a passage. A deeper understanding of Judaism can also help Christians appreciate the human aspect of Jesus. As Martin Buber has said:

> *"We Jews know him [Jesus] in a way - in the impulses and emotions of his essential Jewishness - that remains inaccessible to the Gentiles ...."*[17].

Bachya ben Asher of Saragossa, a Jewish sage who lived in the thirteenth century, noted that there are four ways of interpreting biblical scripture: (a) "P'shat": the literal or plain text explanation of the text, (b) "Remez": the allegorical or symbolic meaning of the text, (c) "Drash", derived from the word "midrash", meaning "interpretation", where a deeper non-literal, ethical or moral lesson is divined in the text, and (d) "Sod": the mystical or secret meaning of the text. The four methods of scriptural analysis are sometimes represented by the acronym of *"pardess"*[18]. Two of the greatest Torah commentators were Rabbi Shlomo Yitzchaki, popularly known as Rashi, an Ashkenazic Jew who lived in Northern France (1040-1104) and Rabbi Moses ben Nachman, popularly known as Nachmanides or Ramban, a Sephardic Jew who lived in Spain (1194-1274). Rashi was known for his terse but pithy "p'shat" - plain text explanations (with some "drash" and "remez" commentaries), while Ramban's commentary explored more deeply the "drash", "remez" and "sod" explanations of the biblical text.

As an example of Rashi's approach, the following is his commentary on Exodus 20:11:

> *"**He blessed...and He sanctified it**. Rashi: He blessed it [the Sabbath] through the manna by giving a double portion on the sixth day - "double bread"; and He sanctified it through the manna in that on it none fell."*

Avigdor Bonchek[19] explains that Rashi by his "Drash" explanation gives an objective manifestation of God's blessing and sanctification by focusing on the manna. On any day other than Friday, if an Israelite were to try to save a double portion of the manna, it turned wormy and rotten (see Exodus 16:20), but on Friday, the Israelites kept a double portion of manna, eating one portion on Friday and saving one portion for Saturday. This second portion of manna did not turn rotten, but was still fresh on the next day. Thus the Sabbath day was blessed and different from other days. The Sabbath day was further "sanctified" or "holy" in that it was separated from the other days of the week, since no work gathering manna would be done - the people did not work for their bread on that day.

An example which may give a sense of Ramban's style of textual analysis is the first line of Exodus **"In the Beginning..."** Rashi in his commentary raises the question as to why the Torah, a collection of commandments (*Mitzvot*), does not begin instead with its first commandment - "This month shall be unto you the beginning of months; it shall be the first month of the year to you" (Exodus 12:2 [Sinai Tanakh]). Ramban quotes this in his commentary and answers the question, stating:

> *"Indeed there is a great need to begin the Torah with 'In the beginning G-d created' because this is the root of our faith. He who does not believe in this and thinks that the world is eternal (i.e. was never created) is a denier of the main [tenet of Jewish belief] and he has no [part in] the Torah."*

The work that follows is a combination of prose and textual commentary on both Jewish scripture and New Testament scripture in the tradition of Rashi and Ramban. Instead of rejecting rabbinic scriptural analysis as has been the usual custom with Christian biblical commentators, I have attempted to utilize these techniques in order to achieve a more nuanced Christian scriptural analysis[20].

The first scriptural commentary in this book is "*Song of Ascents*", which explores the passage in Luke 2:29-32 where Simeon recognizes the infant Jesus at the Temple as "a light for revelation to the Gentiles, and for the glory to thy people Israel." The prose piece is in a form of a "*Drash*" in that it describes Joseph and Mary's pilgrimage to the Temple and the services as they may have existed at the time of the Second Temple to answer the question "what meaningful sign may have been given to Simeon, a devout Jew, so that he would immediately know that Jesus was the one he sought?". The piece is meant to show Christian readers that a deeper understanding of Judaism can add significantly to a Christian's appreciation of New Testament scriptures and recognition of how inextricably linked Christianity is to Judaism.

"Song of Ascents" may also be the most important part of this book since it brings to life for the reader the sacrificial rituals of the Second Temple. I believe these rituals are critical to understanding the meaning of Jesus' ministry during his life and the meaning to Christians of his death and resurrection. I believe it is also critical to appreciating the significance of the prayers and other rituals of worship later developed by Rabbinic Judaism[21]. As Rabbi Neil Gillman has written[22]:

> "*In reality, we modern Jews don't quite know how to deal with the institution of the Temple as a whole, its priestly and Levite classes, its rituals and sacrifices. We tend to see all of this as an ancient practice, and we are secretly grateful that it has never been renewed. Reform and Reconstructionist prayerbooks omit references to sacrifices and to Kohanim and Levites, and Conservative prayerbooks transform the sacrificial passages from a prayer for their restoration (as it appears in all traditional prayerbooks) to a remembrance of what was done in the past. But this evasion is shortsighted...the Temple itself for centuries was our central religious institution, and sacrifices were our ancestors' distinctive mode of worship. Liturgical prayer was a relatively later development, following the destruction of the Second Temple...My colleague Rabbi Ira Stone, in his <u>Seeking the Path to Life</u> tries to recapture the theological underpinnings of the sacrificial rite. He suggests that through the sacrifices, we 'imagine our own death and, yet, go on living. No other form or worship can bring a person so near to the prospect of death.' We intuitively dread death, but in the sacrifice, death becomes our gift to God. 'But death shared with God is no longer death, for there is no death in God.'*"[23]

The second piece, "*Sign of Jonah*", is a commentary on the passage in Luke 11:29, where Jesus likens his mission to Jonah's mission to the Gentiles of Ninevah. The "Sign of Jonah" commentary is meant to show Jewish readers that a scriptural thread runs through the

New Testament which clearly identifies Jesus as "a light for revelation to the Gentiles", not as a sign that God's original covenant with His chosen people, Israel, had been superseded or annulled. It also seeks to confirm the position that Christianity is a monotheistic faith, worshipping the God of Israel. "Sign of Jonah" also utilizes the sacrificial rituals of the Second Temple to more fully explain the significance of the teachings and acts of Jesus.

The third piece is "*Dominion*", which explores how a first century follower of Jesus, familiar with the Temple sacrificial rituals, would have understood the voluntary sacrifice and death of Jesus. It further examines why Judaism and Christianity represent one faith in the worship of the God of Israel, but remain two separate religions -with Ecclesiastes 8:8 being the critical pivot point of their division. It also seeks to explain why it may be God's will that the "fire" of Judaism and the "living waters" of Christianity remain distinct and separate in order to sanctify His great name. Finally, the piece seeks to show that Christians asking themselves "What would Jesus do?" as a guide to how to live their lives would be better able to answer that question if they fully understood the Jewish context within which Jesus lived and preached.

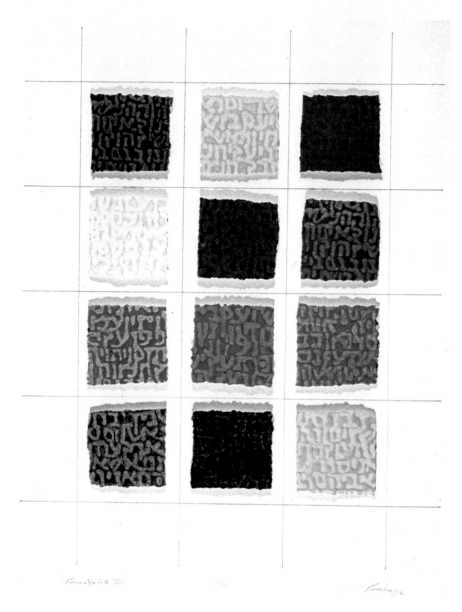

"Aaron's Breastplate"

Exodus describes Aaron's priestly garments in elaborate detail. One translation reads that they were "for beauty and for glory". He wore a breastplate inset with twelve stones inscribed with the names of the twelve tribes of Israel. In this piece, not only are the names inscribed in the Hebrew, but the Genesis text which tells of Jacob blessing his twelve sons is written into the individual collagraphs attached to the background paper. The breastplate was worn as Aaron entered the Holy of Holies, symbolically carrying the nation of Israel into the presence of God. The High Priest wore this breastplate in the Second Temple. Collagraph assemblage 1983 40" x 30" – Sandra Bowden

SONG OF ASCENTS: PSALMS OF DEGREES FOR THE PILGRIMAGE TO JERUSALEM

"Song for the Journey"

Pilgrimage and journey point to a spiritual reconciliation and inner
reconnection. The scallop shell was worn by medieval pilgrims as they trod the
ancient paths to holy destinations. This collage incorporates a page of early lute
music buried beneath layers of thin papers and overlaid with gilded Hebrew text.
As Jewish pilgrims made their way up the hills to the Second Temple in
Jerusalem they sang songs of ascent. Collage mixed media with gold leafing 2000
14.5" x 10.5" - Sandra Bowden

SONG OF ASCENTS:
PSALMS OF DEGREES FOR THE
PILGRIMAGE TO JERUSALEM

"Lord, now lettest thou thy servant depart in peace,
according to thy word; for mine eyes have seen thy salvation
which thou hast prepared in the presence of all peoples,
a light for revelation to the Gentiles,
and for the glory to thy people Israel."[24]

-Luke 2:29-32
[Words of Simeon as Jesus is
presented at the Temple]

[This work seeks to describe the events of the day Jesus was presented at the Temple (the Second Temple in Jerusalem), based on then-current Temple practices, in order to answer the question: what sign might have been given by God to Simeon at the Temple so that he would know that the infant Jesus was the one he sought? It is also designed to evoke Joseph and Mary's pilgrimage into Jerusalem and to relate the story of their pilgrimage to the selected verses from the Song of Ascents (Psalms 120-134), which pilgrims traditionally sang on the way up to Jerusalem and which the Levites also sang during services in the Temple. Hopefully, it will create a tableau in the reader's mind of what I imagine occurred in the Temple in Jerusalem on the day when Mary offered her sacrifice of turtledoves and redeemed Jesus as her firstborn and Simeon recognized him as the "light for revelation to the Gentiles, and for the glory to thy people Israel".]

I
(Psalm 120)

"In my distress I cried unto the Lord, and he heard me...
Woe is me, that I sojourn in Meshech,
that I dwell in the tents of Kedar!
My soul hath long dwelt with him that hateth peace...."[25]

Imagine the family of Joseph and Mary living far from the holy city of Jerusalem in the town of Nazareth, in Galilee (historically the "District of Gentiles")[26], living in the midst of Jews and Gentiles, when Jesus is born. Having given birth to a male child, Mary was ritually impure[27] for seven days. On the eighth day, Jesus is circumcised and for an additional thirty-three days after giving birth, Mary may not approach the sanctuary of the Temple[28]. Only after the specified waiting period may she go to the Temple to make her offerings. As is specified in Leviticus 12:6:

> *"And when the days of her purifying are completed, whether for a son or a daughter, she shall bring to the priest at the door of the tent of meeting a lamb a year old for a burnt offering, and a young pigeon or a turtledove for sin offering, and he shall offer it before the Lord, and make atonement for her; then she shall be clean from the flow of her blood...And if she cannot afford a lamb, then she shall take two turtledoves or two young pigeons, one for a burnt offering and one for a sin offering."*

Also, since Jesus was the firstborn son, his parents are required to redeem him at the Temple by presenting him before the Priests and paying five silver coins (shekels or *Sela'im*) against his redemption, as required in Numbers 18:15-16.

II
(Psalm 121)

> *"...The Lord is thy keeper: the Lord*
> *is thy shade upon thy right hand.*
> *The sun shall not smite me by day*
> *nor the moon by night...."*

Joseph and Mary set out with their infant son, Jesus, on their pilgrimage to the Temple in Jerusalem in order to make Mary's burnt offering and sin offering and to redeem Jesus as the firstborn son. They are not concerned for their home and the carpentry tools and ornamental wooden chest Joseph has almost finished for one of his customers, for it is written: "No man shall covet thy land when thou goest up [to appear before the Lord thy God]"[29].

III
(Psalm 122)

> *"I was glad when they said unto me,*
> *Let us go into the house of the Lord"*

Joseph and Mary talk with fellow pilgrims on the road to Jerusalem, explaining the purpose of their journey. As the day progresses, Joseph plays his wooden flute and Mary sings psalms with their fellow pilgrims as they walk. Joseph teases Mary (whose name is "Miriam" in Hebrew) that he is relying on her to pick out the best springs and watering spots on their journey to Jerusalem, reminding her of Miriam's Rock, which followed the Israelites in the wilderness and provided them with water. Mary feigns anger at Joseph's teasing, so he quotes to her from Song of Songs (Song of Solomon) 7:2 [Koren Tanakh], where it is written "How beautiful are thy feet in sandals, O Prince's daughter" and they link arms as they walk.

IV
(Psalm 123)

"Unto thee lift I up mine eyes,
O thou that dwellest in the heavens ...
Have mercy upon us, O Lord ...."

Traveling on the road to Jerusalem can be hazardous due to the risk of attacks from brigands. Joseph scans the horizon and the neighboring landscape warily for any sign of danger.

V
(Psalm 124)

"... If it had not been the Lord
who was on our side,
when men rose up against us:
Then they had swallowed us up quick,
when their wrath was kindled against us:
... Our soul is escaped as a bird
out of the snare of the fowlers:
the snare is broken, and we are escaped ...."

Joseph and a few of his fellow pilgrims fight off some roadside robbers with their staffs and then give thanks to God for their victory as they proceed on their way with their families.

VI
(Psalm 125)

"... As the mountains are round about Jerusalem,
so the Lord is round about his people
from henceforth even for ever ...
Do good, O Lord, unto those that be good,
and to them that are upright in their hearts ...."

Mary and Joseph leave the mountains of Ephraim behind them and see Jerusalem to the south of them at last, partially obscured by Bezita Hill, with the sun glinting off of the white lime plaster walls of the Temple near the peak of Mount Moriah, with Mount Zion to the west of the Temple and the Mount of Olives to the east of it. They know that the Hinnom Valley to the west and south of Mount Moriah and the Kidron Valley to the east of Mount Moriah meet south of the Old City of David, so that the Temple and the Old City of David stand like a mountain fortress, looking down the steep valley walls to the west, south and east, with only the northwest portion of Mount Moriah connecting directly to the flat mainland. Joseph knows that this northwest portion of the Temple area is where the territory of the tribe of Judah intrudes in a triangular-shaped wedge into the territory of the tribe of Benjamin, fulfilling the scriptures: "And He shall dwell between his shoulders" (Deuteronomy 33:12).[30] The pilgrims sing out praise and thanks to God for their safe journey.

VII
(Psalm 126)

"... They that sow in tears shall reap in joy.
He that goeth forth and weepeth,
bearing precious seed,
shall doubtless come again with rejoicing,
bringing his sheaves with him."

Joseph thinks to himself of the difficult times he and Mary had already gone through and how fortunate they are to have been blessed with a son chosen by God, as the Angel told Joseph, "to save people from their sins" (Matthew 1:21). That is why Mary and Joseph named him "Yeshua" - Jesus - which means "salvation".

VIII
(Psalm 127)

"Except the Lord build the house,
they labour in vain that build it:
except the Lord keep the city,
the watchman waketh but in vain ...."

Joseph, Mary and Jesus arrive at Jerusalem early Friday afternoon, a few hours before the start of the Shabbat [Sabbath] and enter the City of Jerusalem with their fellow pilgrims. They sing again the words from Psalm 122:2: "I was glad when they said unto me, Let us go into the

House of the Lord: When our feet stood within thy gates, O Jerusalem". They greet the watchmen at the gate, comforted that they had reached safety from the dangers of the road, but mindful that even Jerusalem is not safe, if not bound by faith to God and living under His law. Their concerns are laid at rest as they hear shouts from city residents passing them in the street of "Brethren of Galilee, ye come in peace; welcome! Ye come in peace, ye bring peace, and peace be upon you!" [31]

IX

(Psalm 128)

> *"Blessed is every one that feareth the Lord;*
> *that walketh in his ways ...*
> *Thy wife shall be as a fruitful vine*
> *by the sides of thine house:*
> *thy children like olive plants round around thy table ...."*

Joseph speaks earnestly with an innkeeper, seeking a room for his family for the night, explaining the purpose of their pilgrimage and their lack of funds to pay the asking price for the room, most of their shekels being needed for the Temple offering. The innkeeper is impressed that such a poor family would bring five silver coins and two turtledoves to the Temple in order to fulfill their religious obligations. The innkeeper refuses to accept Joseph's offer of a lesser price for the room, and instead offers the room for free, saying that no man has ever said to his fellow "There is no room for me to lodge overnight in Jerusalem", and that he would not be the one to break that tradition.[32] In thanks, Joseph and Mary invite the innkeeper and his family to share their Sabbath dinner with them and their invitation is accepted. After Mary and Joseph have bought food for their Sabbath dinner and have settled themselves in their room, they hear the trumpet sounding three times from the Temple Mount announcing the start of the Shabbat (the Sabbath)[33].

X

(Psalm 129)

> *"... Many a time have they afflicted me from my youth:*
> *yet they have not prevailed against me ...*
> *Neither do they which go by say,*
> *The blessing of the Lord be upon you..."*

The next day, an old man named Simeon, who was born and had lived his entire life in Jerusalem, leaves the Temple ("*Beit Hamikdash*" or "*Beit Yahweh*") after the Saturday afternoon

("*Mincha*") services which end Shabbat (the Sabbath). Simeon passes through the Temple's Eastern Gate, which faces the Shushan Gate in the outer wall of the Temple Mount, leading out over the arched bridge crossing the Kidron Valley to the Mount of Olives to the east. The services had begun a few hours earlier at the ninth hour [*i.e., around 3:00 p.m. in the afternoon*] and as is usual at this time of day, a gusting wind has picked up. It has become cooler on the Temple Mount[34], so Simeon rearranges his outer cloak around his shoulders for more warmth. The melodies of the Song at the Sea and the Song of Moses, which traditionally are sung during the Shabbat afternoon *Mincha* service[35] are still ringing in Simeon's ears:

> *"I will sing unto the Lord, for he hath triumphed gloriously: the horse and his rider hath he thrown into the sea. The Lord is my strength and song, and he is become my salvation: he is my God, and I will prepare him an habitation; my father's God, and I will exalt him...Pharaoh's chariots and his host hath he cast into the sea: his chosen captains also are drowned in the Red Sea...Thy right hand, O Lord, is become glorious in power...And with the blast of thy nostrils the waters were gathered together, the floods stood upright as an heap, and the depths were congealed in the heart of the sea...Thou in thy mercy hast led forth the people which thou has redeemed: thou hast guided them in thy strength unto thy holy habitation...The Lord shall reign for ever and ever...."*: **Song at the Sea** (Exodus 15:1-19)[36]

> *"Give ear, O ye heavens, and I will speak; and hear, O earth, the words of my mouth. My doctrine shall drop as the rain, my speech shall distil as the dew, as the small rain upon the tender herb, and as the showers upon the grass: Because I will publish the name of the Lord: ascribe ye greatness unto our God. He is the Rock, his work is perfect: for all his ways are judgment: a God of truth and without inequity, just and right is he ... Remember the days of old, consider the years of many generations: ask thy father, and he will shew thee; thy elders, and they will tell thee. When the most High divided to the nations their inheritance, when he separated the sons of Adam, he set the bounds of the people according to the number of the children of Israel ... See now that I [the Lord], even I, am he, and there is no god with me: I kill, and I make alive; I wound, and I heal: neither is there any that can deliver out of my hand. For I lift up my hand to heaven, and say, I live for ever ... Rejoice, O ye nations, with his people: for he will avenge the blood of his servants, and will render vengeance to his adversaries, and will be merciful unto his land, and to his people."* : **Song of Moses** (Deuteronomy 32:1-43) [Sinai Tanakh]

Simeon looks back at the 115 foot high Eastern Gate to admire the beauty of the doors. The two doors at the Eastern Gate of the Temple itself are made of richly ornamented Corinthian brass covered in gold and silver and are so massive that it takes 20 Levites to open and close them[37] [*the Levites assist the Priests by singing and playing instruments, and maintain the outer areas of the Temple area*]. Simeon then remembers with reverence and delight the weeklong services he attended at the last Feast of Tabernacles (Sukkot) celebrating the Fall harvest. This is the most important of the three pilgrimage festivals, festivals where all able-bodied Jews are required to journey to the Temple in Jerusalem (the other two being Pesach (Passover) and Shavuot (originally celebrating the Pentecost or "Feast of Weeks" - the feast of the harvest and the day of the first fruits, and later celebrating the giving of the Torah to the Israelites at Mount Sinai[38]).

Indeed, Simeon knew that the seven day Feast of Booths or Tabernacles (Sukkot) was referred to in scripture simply as "ha-Hag" (*"the festival"*) (1 Kings 8:2, 12:32). As commanded in Leviticus 23:40, the worshippers would bring their *Etrog* (a yellow, sweet smelling fruit looking like an oversized lemon and possibly representing the forbidden fruit that Eve and Adam ate in the Garden of Eden) and the *Lulav* (date palm leaves, willow branches and myrtle branches tied together), with them to the Temple. The worshippers would hold the Etrog in their left hand and the Lulav in their right hand and shake the Lulav to the west in the direction of the stone altar, which was covered with date palm branches, but also north, east and south, up and down. The Great Hallel (Psalms 113-118), which were psalms of praise (*Hallel*) were said every day at the Temple during the seven day festival. Over the seven day period, the Priests sacrificed 70 bulls in atonement for the sins of the 70 nations of the world and each day they poured water from the Pool of Siloam on the stone altar. While at the other two pilgrimage festivals (Pesach and Shavuot), the agricultural cycle of the year was still in full stride, at Sukkot this cycle was completed. Accordingly, the festival lasted for seven days and an eighth day festival, *Shemini Atzeret*, was celebrated where one bull was sacrificed at the Temple for Israel alone, in the belief that God had implored the Jewish nation to spend one more day with Him [Numbers 29:35 and Ecclesiastes 11:12]. In remembrance of the years spent in the wilderness, Jews built booths or tabernacles (Sukkot) with open, latticed roofs covered with straw and leaves and would live and eat meals in them, under the stars. The Jews living in Jerusalem built their booths in the Temple square. Finally, in each *Shemittah* year (the seventh year of each seven year cycle, which was devoted to God by allowing agricultural lands to lie fallow and performing other acts), the King of Israel would read from the Torah during the Sukkot festival to the entire nation[39] The Temple scroll was kept near the Gate of Nicanor and was rolled around two long wooden rods, each with an ivory pomegranate finial topped by six petals, representing six of the tribes of Israel and bearing the inscription *"Qodes Kohanim l-beyt [Yahwe]h"* ("sacred donation for the priests of the House of Yahweh").[40] The reading of the scroll by the King to the people at Sukkot reminded Simeon of the time when the people stood at the foot of Mount Sinai and received the Torah, *"as one man with one heart.[41]"*

Model of Temple Mount

Model of Second Temple

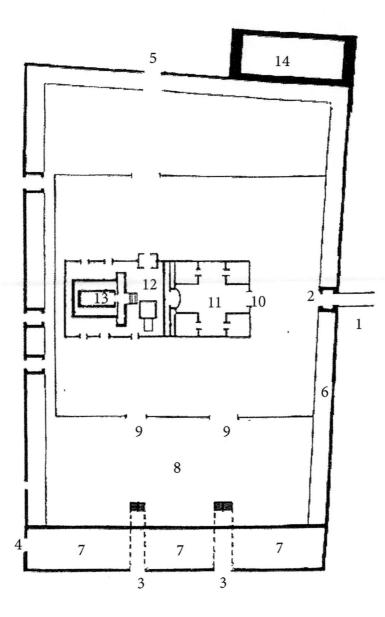

Diagram of the Temple Mount

1. Bridge over the Valley of Kidron, from the Mount of Olives **2**. Shushan Gate **3**. Huldah Gates **4**. Robinson's Arch (entrance to Basilica) **5**. Tadi Gate **6**. Solomon's Porch **7**. Basilica and Royal Porch **8**. Courtyard of the Gentiles **9**. Soreq (Wall of Partition) **10**. Eastern Gate **11**. Courtyard of the Women **12**. Courtyard of the Priests **13**. Holy of Holies **14**. Sheep Pool

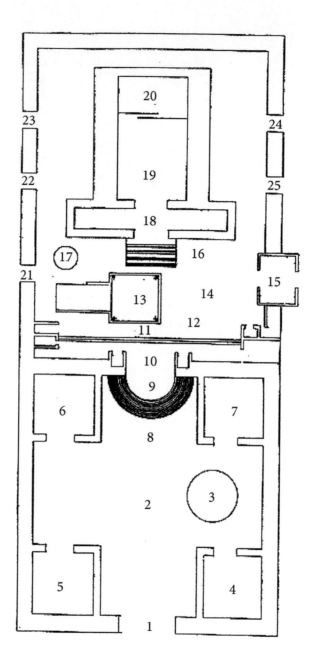

Diagram of the Second Temple

1. Eastern Gate **2**. Courtyard of the Women **3**. Sanhedria Katanah **4**. Chamber of Wood **5**. Chamber of Nazarites **6**. Chamber of Oil **7**. Chamber of the Lepers **8**. 15 Steps Where the Levites Sang the Song of Ascents **9**. Gate of Nicanor **10**. Courtyard of the Israelites **11**. Duchan **12**. Courtyard of the Priests **13**. Stone Altar **14**. Area for Sacrifices, Containing 24 Rings, Tables and Pillars **15**. Chamber of the Hearth **16**. Courtyard of the Priests **17**. Kiyor **18**. Sanctuary Entrance Hall **19**. Sanctuary Holding the Shulchan with Shewbread, the Golden Menorah and the Golden Altar **20**. Holy of Holies **21**. Water Gate **22**. Gate of the Firstborn **23**. Gate of the Firewood **24**. Gate of Sacrifice **25**. Spark Gate

All night long at the close of the first day of the festival of Sukkot, Simeon remembers singing and dancing with other Israelites in the open air Women's Courtyard just inside the Eastern Gate. The Women's Courtyard is a square space approximately 200 feet long on each side which was given its name because women normally would not proceed any closer to the open air altar in front of the Sanctuary building unless they were making a sacrifice[42]. The memory of the nighttime scene at the Feast of Tabernacles (Sukkot) remains very vivid for Simeon, as he pictures it once more in his mind:

The open air Women's Courtyard was lit by the flickering lights of four gigantic candelabra, each having five oil-filled wicks, which required the Levites to use tall ladders in order to fill them. A few of the pious men and "men of deed" juggled burning torches in the air to the delight of the women leaning over the temporary balconies running around the top of the inner wall of the Women's Courtyard, set up for this very festival[43].

As the dawn approached, two Priests stood in the Courtyard of the Priests where the massive open air stone altar stood. The two Priests advanced eastward across the small Courtyard of the Israelites through the Gate of Nicanor and down the fifteen semi-circular stone steps leading to the Women's Courtyard. The Levites played harps, lutes, and cymbals while standing upon the fifteen steps leading down from the Courtyard of Priests to the Women's Courtyard. The fifteen steps match the fifteen Songs of Ascent (or Degrees)(Psalms 120-134)[44].

The Song of Ascents (Shir ha-Maalot), sung by the Levites on the fifteen steps which pilgrims ascend to make their sacrifices during the daily services, remind Simeon of the increasing degrees of holiness within the Temple area. The degrees of holiness are lowest out in the Courtyard of the Gentiles and increase through the Courtyard of Women, Courtyard of the Israelites, Courtyard of Priests, the golden altar for incense in the front of the Sanctuary and finally culminate in the highest degree of holiness behind the curtains shielding the Holy of Holies in the back of the Sanctuary. There in the Holy of Holies, the degree of holiness was so great that the High Priest alone could enter it and even then only once each year on the Day of Atonement (Yom Kippur)[45].

As the cock crowed to announce the dawn, the two Priests started to blow their silver trumpets three times at the top step of the fifteen steps. The three trumpet sounds - a "tekiah", a "teruah" and then a "tekiah" (a short sharp note, followed by a longer alarm, and finally another short sharp note) symbolically proclaimed the kingdom of God, Divine Providence and the final judgment[46]. The Priests then walked down five more steps and blew the trumpets another three times, progressing until they reach the Women's Courtyard. Crossing that courtyard to the Eastern Gate, the two Priests turned fully around and faced west.

The Priests looked up past the fifteen steps leading through the Gate of Nicanor to the Courtyard of the Israelites, past the open air stone altar in the Courtyard of Priests to the tall building housing the Entrance Hall and the Sanctuary. Beyond the Entrance Hall were the golden doors leading to the Sanctuary, flanked on either side by tall pillars supporting large cedar beams. Affixed to the 30 ton stone lintel above the gateway to the Sanctuary is one of the symbols of Israel, a gigantic grape vine of pure gold, from which hang golden leaves and berry clusters as large as a man, given as votive offerings (Psalm 80:9 [Sinai Tanakh]- "Thou hast brought a vine [Israel] out of Egypt").

The worshippers' eyes were fixed on the Temple building. On the top of the building sit golden spikes to keep birds from landing on the roof and these spikes have begun to glisten from the rising sun. The Temple building is the size of a 17 story building, built with the Entrance Hall wider in front than the Sanctuary behind it, so that the entire Temple building sits like a lion in the Courtyard of the Priests[47]. The outer walls of the Temple building were made with blue-green marble, with wide strips of white marble covered with white lime plaster fixed in horizontal rows over the blue-green marble, leaving only thin strips of the blue-green marble showing, so that no one could touch the actual Temple walls. Although Herod had wished to put gold plate over the outer walls, the Priests had requested instead that he leave the simple alternating blue-green and white surface, since in the sun it shimmers like the waves of the sea.[48]

The dawn had been blocked so far by the high eastern Temple walls, but as the assembled worshippers saw the Temple walls begin to shimmer white, with hints of sea-green, and then see the sunlight begin to reflect off the golden candelabrum hanging from the doorway of the Entrance Hall, they knew that dawn had fully arrived[49]. The two Priests then said in voices loud enough to be heard by all:

"Our fathers who were in this place, they turned their back upon the Sanctuary of Jehovah, and their faces toward the east, and they worshipped towards the rising sun; but as for us, our eyes are toward the Lord."[50]

The two Priests then turned to one another and said:

"The Lord bless thee out of Zion; and see thou the good of Jerusalem all the days of thy life; and see thy children's children. Peace be upon Israel!"[51]

The memory passes and Simeon is brought suddenly back to the present as his elbow is

26

jostled by another worshipper leaving the Temple. Simeon reluctantly puts aside the image of the Sukkot festival, but is comforted, since he knows that in the future messianic time, all of the nations will come up to Jerusalem to worship the God of Israel in the Temple and celebrate the Feast of Tabernacles (Sukkot)[52].

Walking down the steps of the Temple, which is built on a foundation of solid blocks of white marble, Simeon proceeds toward the Wall of Partition (the "Soreg"). This 4 1/2 foot high marble balustrade separates the 500 cubit square Temple area (which only a Jew may enter) from the Courtyard of the Gentiles, an immense open area paved in white, brown and bluish-purple variegated marble[53], which is open to Gentiles as well as Jews. Simeon proceeds across the open air Courtyard of the Gentiles, passing the two cisterns of water carved into the courtyard and reserved for the purification of Jewish Temple worshippers prior to their entering the Temple area. Simeon proceeds further and pauses behind a crowd of worshippers descending the rightmost of two staircases leading underground to a passageway ending in a "double gate", one of the two Huldah Gates named after the prophetess Huldah. The Huldah Gates open out onto a plaza overlooking the old City of David to the south of the Temple Mount.

Instead of proceeding underground with the crowd, Simeon turns right and exits the Courtyard of the Gentiles through the Coponius Gate to the West. Then Simeon walks along the road bordering the Western Wall of the Temple, paved with large rectangular stones. Shops line the western Temple Mount wall and Simeon glances at some of the goods for sale. Simeon reenters the Temple Mount by ascending the stairs to the south, through an arch [*now called Robinson's Arch*] into the Royal Porch. The Royal Porch runs along the southernmost area of the Temple Mount and houses the basilica, dedicated to money-changing and banking activities. Simeon has to exit the Temple Mount and reenter it via another gate to the south because the Basilica in the Royal Porch does not have any gates opening onto the Courtyard of the Gentiles on the Temple Mount[54].

The Royal Porch is a three level colonnaded stoa (a long hall with a central nave) formed of 162 white marble pillars, each 37 ½ feet high[55], with the bottom nave being 45 feet wide and the entire structure being approximately 912 feet long [56]. Like the rest of the Temple, the Royal Porch was designed in the Corinthian architectural style and each pillar of the stoa is so large that three men surrounding the pillar with arms outstretched could barely touch each others' fingers. The ceilings of the Stoa are paneled in fine cedar, which stands out in sharp contrast to the white marble. Simeon walks up the staircases of the Royal Porch until he reaches the top. Out of breath and feeling very old, Simeon stops and looks back at the Temple from the 150 foot height of the top level of the Royal Porch, as was his custom at the end of each Sabbath. The purple light of sunset is just starting to fade on the mountains of Moab far to the East. Looking north and east over the Courtyard of Gentiles, the Wall of Partition and beyond it to the Temple itself, with a greater expanse of the Courtyard of Gentiles beyond the northern side of the Temple area, Simeon is awed as he always was at the vast expanse of the Temple Mount. Simeon has heard travelers report that the Temple Mount, being comprised of an area of approximately 145 acres[57], is five times the size of the Parthenon.

The Temple Mount has five gates, the two gates of Huldah to the south, the gate of Coponius on the west and the gate of Taddi on the north which did not have a normal lintel but rather two stones inclined against one another and which was not used by the public. Simeon looks over to his right to the fifth gate, the Shushan Gate, leading to the bridge spanning the Valley of Kidron, and pictures in his mind the bas relief above the Shushan Gate which commemorates Shushan, the capital of Persia, which had been the Israelites' home in exile[58]. It is through the Shushan gate [*known as the "Beautiful Gate" (Acts 3:2)*[59]] that the priests would take the red heifer on Yom Kippur, the day of atonement, to the Mount of Olives to be burned. The ashes of the red heifer were then used for purification rituals by the Temple priests.[60] Simeon then remembers that the cubit, the unit of measurement [*approximately 1.7 feet*] on which the original Tabernacle in the wilderness and later the First Temple and current Second Temple was based, was carved into the wall of a room above the Shushan Gate[61].

Simeon imagines that in the messianic age, the messiah ("*Mashiach*") will lead the nations of the world across the great bridge and through the Shushan Gate to worship at the Temple. However, at that time, Simon imagines that the olive tree as the symbol of Israel will replace the cubit above the Shushan Gate as the standard by which all of the nations coming to worship God will be measured to determine if they would be worthy of entrance. Musing on these thoughts, Simeon then starts to walk down the stairs of the Royal Porch, heading home.

The combined smells of the foods of the many nations making up the population of Jerusalem waft up disagreeably to Simeon and the night-time sounds of the city, an unintelligible mixture of Aramaic, Greek, Latin and other languages, grows louder as he leaves the Royal Porch behind. Simeon walks down the massive staircase he had ascended earlier, which makes two right-angle turns to the southwestern base of the Temple Mount buttress wall. Simeon heads south on the stone path and heads toward the Pool of Siloam. Simeon passes numerous pagan Gentiles on his way home to the City of David, but they ignore him and say no greetings, oblivious to the passing of the Sabbath. Simeon wraps the memory of the Temple service about himself like a protective cloak and thinks regretfully to himself that he would likely not live to see the day that every nation would come to Jerusalem to worship the God of Israel.

It saddens Simeon, who imagines the glory of that day, when all sin will have been eliminated and virtue will fill the world. Then, the glory of God will replace the sun and moon as the light of the world and the Sin Offerings and similar penitential sacrificial offerings at the

Temple will be abolished, except for the Thanksgiving Offering of loaves of bread[62] and the only prayers will be prayers of thanksgiving[63], especially Psalm 100 [Sinai Tanakh]:

"A psalm of thanksgiving: Make a joyful noise unto the Lord, all ye lands. Serve the Lord with gladness: come before his presence with singing. Know ye that the Lord he is God: it is he that hath made us, and we belong unto him; we are his people, and the sheep of his pasture. Enter into his gates [e.g., Eastern Gate or one of the other nine gates of the Temple] with thanksgiving, and into his courts [e.g., Court of the Women and Court of the Israelites] with praise: be thankful unto him, and bless his name. For the Lord is good; his mercy is everlasting; and his truth endureth to all generations." [explanatory notations in italics added]

XI
(Psalm 130)

"Out of the depths have I cried unto thee, O Lord ...
My soul waiteth for the Lord more
than they that watch for the morning ...."

In the middle of the night, Simeon is given a dream by God which amazes him. Although Simeon is not of priestly descent or even a Levite, but just an Israelite, Simeon dreams that he is ascending the steps to the Sanctuary and approaching the golden altar. As he stands in front of the altar, incense begins to burn and a fiery angel, of terrifying visage, appears to the right side of the altar. Simeon is frightened and falls prostrate on the floor, certain that he will be destroyed immediately for being within the Sanctuary[64]. Instead, the angel tells him not to be afraid, for he has been blessed by God. The angel tells Simeon that although he is right that his death is near, Simeon will not see death before he had seen the one who had been chosen to be a revelation to the Gentiles, to the glory of Israel. Simeon awakes in a sweat, uncertain as to whether to believe the dream or not. Unable to sleep any longer, Simeon paces by his window looking out on a narrow, winding street of the City of David, hopeful that the next day's Temple services would reveal the truth of his dream. Simeon is concerned, however, because the dream did not show him any sign by which to recognize the chosen one.

XII
(Psalm 131)

"Lord, my heart is not haughty,
nor mine eyes lofty ...
Surely I have behaved and quieted myself,

as a weaned child beside his mother:
my soul within me
is even as a weaned child...."

Simeon stands in the Women's Courtyard listening to the Sunday morning ("*Shacharit*") service in the Temple, the service for the first day of the week. Simeon prays silently to God for the calm patience to wait all that day and succeeding days, if necessary, for the sign that his dream was a true vision from God. A number of Temple money chests in the shape of inverted trumpets (*shofarot*)[65] line the Women's Courtyard for purposes of those worshippers wishing to make offerings: six trumpets marked for "Freewill Offerings", two for "New Shekels" [shekels due each year] and "Old Shekels" [for shekels due the prior year but not yet paid], one trumpet for "Gold for the Mercy Seat", one for "Wood" and three trumpets for various types of sacrifices ("*korbonot*") - "Frankincense", "Bird Offerings" [turtledoves], and "Young Birds for Whole Offerings" [pigeons].[66] There was no money chest for obligatory bird offerings[67]. Simeon has already placed his offering in one of the six "Freewill Offering" trumpets.

In front of Simeon, the semi-circular stone staircase of fifteen steps leads up to the sixty foot high Nicanor Gate and the small Courtyard of the Israelites. To either side of the bottommost of the fifteen steps are doors leading from the Courtyard of Women down to chambers holding the musical instruments of the Levites. The Courtyard of the Israelites at the top of the fifteen steps is a 16 1/2 feet long rectangular space at the Gate of Nicanor which itself opens onto steps leading up into the Courtyard of Priests (the "*Azarah*") where the offerings of burnt animal sacrifices and sacrifices of grain and wine are made on the large stone altar, which does not sit on marble, but rests on the bedrock of Mount Moriah itself.

Simeon looks up at the doors of the Nicanor Gate, the only gateway doors in the Temple not covered in gold or silver and the only gateway in the Temple to have a mezuzah[68], and remembers standing as a boy in the Temple with his father while his father told him the story of the door. As Simeon's father recounted, a man named Nicanor was sent to Alexandria to pick up two copper doors and bring them back to Jerusalem for installation at the Temple. During the voyage, however, a terrible storm arose and the sailors threw one of the doors overboard to lighten the load. When the sailors went to throw the second door overboard, Nicanor held fast to the door and said to throw him overboard with the door. The sailors left Nicanor and the remaining door alone and the storm subsided. A miracle occurred when the ship reached the shore, for they found the second door floating alongside the ship. In honor of this, the two doors were mounted at the Nicanor Gate and were in their original state, without any gold or silver overlays[69].

Simeon smiles at the memory of his beloved father, long since passed away. For a year after his father's death, Simeon had gone to the Temple every day to offer prayers on his father's behalf, should his father's soul have been sent to *Gehenna* as a result of earthly sins. On the first anniversary of his death, Simeon knew, his father's soul (*"neshama"*) was freed to ascend to the treasury of souls[70] to wait for the Day of Judgment and the resurrection, when his father's resurrected body and soul would be reunited.

As he puts the memory of his father aside, Simeon looks up past the stone altar at the Sanctuary building further west of the Courtyard of the Priests. There a second, smaller altar, made of gold rather than of stone, stood within the Sanctuary building (the *"Heichal"*) for offerings of incense to accompany the prayers during the services. One fortunate priest chosen by lot is already preparing the incense for burning on coals on the golden altar for that morning's service[71], while another has finished trimming the wicks for five of the lamps in the seven-branched candelabrum (*"Menorah"*) on the southern wall of the Sanctuary [*the remaining two lamps are to be trimmed and replenished with oil after the burning of the incense[72]*]. Simeon knew that the incense for the golden altar was made by the family of Abtinus from thirteen spices and other ingredients, gathered from the land and the sea, from inhabited and uninhabited lands, and mixed according to a secret formula, symbolically representing that all things are from God and for God[73]. As with the animal sacrifices, salt is added to the incense offering.[74]

The front half of the Sanctuary building, which is covered on the inside walls, floor and ceiling with golden tiles, also contains the golden table (*"Shulchan"*) on its northern wall for the Shewbread (twelve loaves to represent the twelve tribes, baked weekly and eaten by the Priests each Sabbath). Simeon knows that the Shewbread is the *"Lechem Hapanim"* - the "face" or very presence of the Lord and that it is as fresh when the Priests eat it on every Shabbat as it was seven days before when it was placed in the Sanctuary[75]. Simeon knows that this is one of the many miracles of the Temple.

Further west in the back half of the Sanctuary building is the Holy of Holies (*"Kodesh HaKedoshim"*), hidden behind two ceiling- length overlapping curtains embroidered with white, blue, scarlet and purple thread depicting the heavens. Simeon imagines that the white thread represents the earth, the blue thread represents air, the scarlet thread represents fire and the purple thread represents the sea[76]. The Holy of Holies, steeped in darkness, had once held the Ark of the Covenant, the staff of Aaron and a jar containing manna during the time of the First Temple, but in the Second Temple it lies empty with the exception of the low Foundation Stone in the exposed bedrock (where Abraham had sacrificed the ram in place of Isaac[77] and on which the Ark had rested). Simeon knows that only in two places in the Temple is the bedrock exposed, here in the Holy of Holies and outside in the Courtyard of the Priests at the stone altar.

XIII
(Psalm 132)

"We will go into his tabernacles:
we will worship at his footstool.
Arise, O Lord, into thy rest; thou,
and the ark of thy strength.
Let thy priests be clothed with righteousness;
and let thy saints shout for joy.
For thy servant David's sake turn
not away the face of thine anointed ...."

That same Sunday morning, Mary and Joseph arise early and approach the Temple Mount from the City of David. At the southern base of the Temple Mount, they enter a low building to their left to immerse themselves in a "*mikveh*", an immersion pool carved into the ground which contains rain water or spring water ("living water"), in order to purify themselves before approaching the Temple Mount. They walk up to the plaza with the monumental steps leading up to the Huldah Gates where a few merchants have set up stands for the sale of turtledoves, pigeons and other necessaries for the sacrifices. Joseph stops at one stand that is selling enclosed offering baskets for those suffering from *Tzara'as* (spiritual leprosy), **each containing a pair of turtledoves, together with red cloth ribbon, cedarwood and hyssop**. Joseph had been looking to purchase just an offering basket with two turtledoves, but the price of these offering baskets is the same - eight *Zuz*[78], so he purchases one of them for Mary.

Those suffering from *Tzara'as* (spiritual leprosy) traditionally give this type of offering to the Priests during their ceremony of purification at the Temple. The Priest would kill one of the turtledoves over "living water", allowing the blood to spill into the water. Then the Priest would tie together the red cloth ribbon with the cedarwood and hyssop and dip them, together with the second, living turtledove, into the bloodstained water. The blood from the living bird then would be sprinkled on the leper and the living bird set free towards the fields[79]. Joseph removes the cedarwood, hyssop and red cloth ribbon from the inside of the offering basket, since Mary will not need them for her offering. **Mary uses the red cloth ribbon to tie the cedarwood and hyssop to the outside of the basket holding Jesus, for safekeeping**.

Joseph and Mary pause to admire the imposing southern wall of the Temple Mount rising 50 meters high. Some of the blocks of stone comprising the wall weigh from two to ten tons each, with the cornerstones weighing approximately 40 to 50 tons. The blocks of stone are chiseled around their edges to give a frame effect, so that from a distance the wall looks like a quilt of stones. At the top of the wall, they see pilasters of stone attached to the outer surface[80]. Joseph and Mary then enter the Huldah Triple Gate, ascending the mighty fifty foot wide staircase and walking up a 295 foot long ascending tunnel. Ancient columns topped with tiers of carved acanthus leaves, dating from the time of the First Temple, support domed ceilings above their heads. The walls and ceilings bear complex geometric designs similar to those of an oriental carpet and also carvings depicting the seven Biblical fruits and grains of the nation of Israel (wheat, barley, [grape] vines, figs, pomegranates, olive trees and [date] honey)[81]. These are the seven species, the first fruits (*Bikkurim*) of which are marked by a piece of straw when they first appear and later are offered as sacrifices at the Temple, starting at the festival of Shavuot, the first fruits festival (the *Hag Ha-Bikkurim*)[82]. Shavuot is also known as the Feast of Weeks because worshippers count 7 weeks or 50 days from Passover, with the Festival of First Fruits as an "Atzeret" or concluding festival for Passover. This period of 50 days [Pentecost] is known as "counting the omer", since grains of wheat are counted to mark each day. The carvings of the seven species cause Joseph and Mary to think back on the last Shavuot festival they had attended:

Mary and Joseph were part of a large group of pilgrims to Jerusalem, with their procession being led by an ox whose horns had been adorned with gold and silver wreaths and with olive branches. Some of the wealthier pilgrims in the group were carrying their first fruits in baskets of silver and gold, while Joseph and Mary and their neighbors had their first fruits in wicker baskets made of peeled willow branches. Some of the pilgrims who lived far from Jerusalem had brought dried fruits. Also, many pilgrims had pigeons perched on top of their baskets, destined for sacrifice at the Temple's altar. Although the sacrifice of first fruits could be made at any time between Shavuot in the late Spring and Sukkot (the Feast of Booths or Tabernacles) in the Fall[83], Joseph and Mary had arrived to participate in the first Shavuot festival.

As the procession reached the Huldah Gate, it was greeted by emissaries from the Temple and all the inhabitants of Jerusalem who were the area stood up in honor of the procession of first fruits[84]. Finally, at the ceremony at the Temple, the Bikkurim and pigeons were offered up as burnt offerings and the worshippers presented their baskets of first fruits to the Priests. Holding the baskets on their shoulders, the worshippers recited the passage "I profess this day unto the Lord thy God, that I am come unto the country which the Lord sware unto our fathers for to give us" [Deuteronomy 26:3][Sinai Tanakh]. Then they removed the baskets from their shoulders and held them by the rim. The Priests put their hands under the worshippers' hands holding their baskets of first fruits and "waved" the baskets back and forth. The worshippers then recited Deuteronomy 26:5-10 (the Mikra Bikkurim)[Sinai Tanakh]:

"A Syrian ready to perish was my father, and he went down into Egypt, and sojourned there with a few, and became there a nation, great, mighty, and populous; And the

Egyptians evil entreated us, and afflicted us, and laid upon us hard bondage; And when we cried unto the Lord God of our fathers, the Lord heard our voice, and looked on our affliction, and our labour, and our oppression; And the Lord brought us forth out of Egypt with a mighty hand, and with an outstretched arm, and with great terribleness, and with signs, and with wonders; And he hath brought us into this place, and hath given us this land, even a land that floweth with milk and honey. And now, behold, I have brought the first-fruits of the land, which thou, O Lord, hast given me."

They placed the baskets by the side of the altar, prostrated themselves and departed[85]. The Priests also offered up two lambs and two loaves of leavened bread (unlike the normal unleavened meal sacrifice) on the altar to mark the end of the grain harvest[86].

Mary and Joseph put aside their recollection of the First Fruits festival as they emerge from the darkness of the tunnel into brilliant sunlight again and pause for a moment in the Courtyard of the Gentiles on the Temple Mount to let their eyes adjust to the light, in awe of the blazing white and gold Temple rising up in front of them. They walk past the signs written in Greek and Latin on the Wall of Partition that warn non-Jews to proceed no further, under pain of death[87]. Mary and Joseph wait with the other worshippers for the three blasts from the Priests' trumpets which announce the beginning of the morning service at the third hour [*around 9:00 am*], at which time the great doors at the nine gates of the Temple are opened by the Levites. Mary and Joseph ascend the twelve steps on the east side of the Temple, passing through the Eastern Gate, the primary entrance to the Temple.

As they enter the Women's Courtyard, they see a Nazarite with long shaggy hair and rough clothing enter the small square roofless building to the left of them, in the southeast corner of the Women's Courtyard. Nazarites undertake a vow to become "*nazar*", separated and holy unto God, by abstaining from wine, from cutting their hair and from touching any dead body (even refraining from burying their own parents if they were to die) for the term of the vow[88]. Some, like Samson [*and John the Baptist in the time of Jesus*], are Nazarites for life. In the Chamber of Nazarites in the Women's Courtyard, the Nazarites cut and burn their hair, cook their peace-offerings and perform the other rituals necessary to end their term as a Nazarite, which Joseph knows is normally a minimum of thirty days.

To the immediate right of them, Mary and Joseph see a priest dressed in black leaving the Chamber of Wood, a second square building located in the northeast corner of the Women's Courtyard, holding an armful of wood destined for the altar[89]. Priests chosen to serve at the sacrificial altar normally wear white vestments. Applicants for Priesthood who are found to be descended from a divorced woman or who were otherwise genealogically "blemished" are not qualified to be full priests. Instead, they wear black vestments and perform other functions within the Temple such as examining sacrificial wood for worms[90]. Joseph remembers hearing that it was suspected that the lost Ark of the Covenant might be hidden beneath the Chamber of Wood[91]. To the west of the Chamber of Wood sits a small enclosed building housing the *Sanhedria Katanah*, a high court of Jewish law comprised of 23 judges, which decided capital cases.[92]

Mary and Joseph then proceed across the Women's Courtyard and see in front of them to the left some Levites taking jars of wine and oil out of the Chamber of Oil, a small square building in the southwest corner of the Women's Courtyard. To their front right, some Israelites suffering from "*Tzara'as*" -spiritual leprosy"[93] - are entering the square Chamber of Lepers in the northwest corner of the Women's Courtyard. There the lepers will immerse themselves in "living water" as part of their purification ceremony[94]. Joseph appreciates why the Chamber of Nazarites is placed on the southern wall (the "right hand of God"), while the Chamber of Lepers is on the opposite wall, but he wonders to himself why the Chamber of the Lepers is placed closer to the Holy of Holies than the Chamber of Nazarites. Joseph wonders if it is because the doorway of the Chamber of Nazarites opens toward the Sanctuary, while the doorway of the Chamber of Lepers opens away from it.

The Priests open the gate to the Sanctuary and the High Priest ("*Kohain Gadol*") sacrifices a lamb to begin the morning service[95]. The sacred fire on the altar sits low on a large pile of wood on the east side of the altar and Joseph remembers that he had heard once that in the time of the First Temple, when the religious stature of the High Priests had been higher, the fire on the altar had been much larger, "crouching like a lion". The smoke from the offering rises in a straight line heavenward.

As the Priests sound their trumpets, Mary and Joseph ascend the fifteen steps leading to the Gate of Nicanor, accompanied by Levites. The Priests then recite the Shema and the Ten Commandments. The Priests also bless the worshippers with three benedictions, which include a blessing acknowledging the holiness of the Priestly line and the obligation of the Priests to bless the people in love[96]. The Priests then place incense and coals from the outer stone altar on the golden altar within the Sanctuary and the High Priest stays inside the Sanctuary to offer up prayers on behalf of the people:

> "...Be graciously pleased, the Lord our God, with Thy people Israel, and with their prayer...We praise Thee, who are the Lord our God, and the God of our fathers, the God of all flesh, our Creator, and the Creator from the beginning! ...So preserve us and keep us, and gather the scattered ones into Thy holy courts...Blessed be Thou, Lord, who blessest Thy people Israel with peace."[97]

Joseph muses to himself that just as a cloud of smoke acted as a protective buffer at the base of Mount Sinai between God and the people of Israel, so the cloud of incense from the golden altar acted as a buffer between the Holy of Holies and the worshippers in the Temple. As the High Priest comes out from the Sanctuary, the Priests stand upon the steps leading into the Sanctuary, lifting up their hands and placing them together in the sign of priestly benediction. The Priests do this by joining their two outspread hands above their heads, making the tips of the fingers touch each other. At the same time, the first and the second fingers, and the third and fourth fingers in each hand are knit together and a division is made between those fingers, spreading them apart. The High Priest holds his hands in the form of blessing, not above his head as the other Priests do, but level with the plate on his head covering which reads "Holiness Unto the Lord"[98]. The High Priest then blesses the worshippers with the benediction from Numbers 6:24-26:

"The Lord bless thee and keep thee: The Lord make His face shine upon thee, and be gracious unto thee: The Lord lift up His countenance upon thee, and give thee peace."

Mary and Joseph, together with the other worshippers, prostrate themselves and say in unison *"Blessed be the Lord God, the God of Israel, from everlasting to everlasting."* Joseph knew that in ancient times, the Priests had actually said the ineffable name of God ("*YHWH*" or "Yahweh"), but now the Name of God was never said, even in the Temple[99]. Instead, one of the seventy names reflecting the various attributes of God (e.g., "Adonai" (Lord)[100], "*Shaddai*" (Omnipotent God), "*Hashem*" (God of Mercy) and "*Elohim*" (God of Judgment)) was used.

At this point in the morning service, the Segan, a Pharisee who acts as Deputy High Priest in order to confirm that the service has been properly conducted by the High Priest, who is a Sadducee, ascends the stone altar. Standing on one of the horns of the altar, the Segan raises a flag as a signal. Two Priests stand on top of the two tables to the west of the stone altar and sound a "Teruah" and a "Tekiah" with trumpets. The Segan waves the flag again and Priests sound cymbals while the High Priest burns the meat and fat from the sacrificial lamb (the *Tamid*)[101]. The High Priest's daily "*Mincha*" offering, comprised of twelve unleavened half-cakes in the shape of wafers[102], are sprinkled with oil, salted and then burned on the altar[103] and the drink offering is poured out at the southwestern corner of the altar[104].

The Temple music then begins, with the Levites playing instruments such as the *nevalim* (a type of lyre*), the kinnor* (a type of harp), the *chalil* (a double pipe wind instrument) and the *tziltzilim* (finger cymbals)[105]. The Levites sing the Psalm of the day, accompanied by the metal trumpets of the Priests. Mary and Joseph stand in the midst of the Priests and Levites at the Gate of Nicanor as they sing the daily Psalm, divided into three sections, with trumpets blown at the pause after the singing of each section. As each "Tekiah" is blown by the trumpet, the worshippers prostrate themselves[106]. The Psalms are chosen to match the seven days of creation and **Psalm 24** [Sinai Tanakh] ("The earth is the Lord's") is sung on Sunday, the first day of the week[107]:

> *"The earth is the Lord's, and the fulness thereof; the world and they that dwell therein.*
> *For he hath founded it upon the seas, and established it upon the floods. Who shall*
> *ascend unto the hill of the Lord? Or who shall stand in his holy place? He that hath*
> *clean hands, and a pure heart; who hath not lifted up his soul unto vanity, nor sworn*
> *deceitfully. He shall receive the blessing from the Lord, and righteousness from the God*
> *of his salvation. This is the generation of them that seek him, that seek thy face, O Jacob.*
> *Selah*[108]*. Lift up your hands, O ye gates; and be ye lift up, ye everlasting doors; and the*
> *King of glory will come in. Who is this King of Glory? The Lord strong and mighty, the*
> *Lord mighty in battle. Lift up your hands, O ye gates; even lift them up, ye everlasting*
> *doors; and the King of Glory shall come in. Who is this King of Glory? The Lord of hosts,*
> *He is the King of glory. Selah"*[109]*.*

Now that the morning service is over, a Priest approaches the graceful 18 inch high stone parapet[110], which, together with a set of three steps, known as the Priests' Platform or "*Duchan*"[111], separates the consecrated ground of the Courtyard of Priests from the unconsecrated Courtyard of the Israelites. The Priest is dressed in his four sacred vestments (white shining linen breeches, a long coat woven of one piece of linen, thrown over his shoulder, a white cloth girdle wrapped around his chest and head covering)[112]. The Temple Priests serve in twenty-four "watches" or shifts[113]. These shifts rotate throughout the religious year, although at the three principal Temple feasts all twenty-four watches are present and serve[114].

The High Priest, standing to the north of the altar, is dressed in eight golden vestments (*Bigdai Zahav*)[115] and has a golden plate tied with blue ribbon around his mitre, which says "Holiness Unto the Lord"[116]. His robes, designed "for honor and for beauty" (Exodus 28:2), are girded about by a sash of five bands of color: gold, purple, scarlet, white and blue, the same colors used on the two overlapping curtains guarding the Holy of Holies[117]. On the bottom of his robe are golden bells and blue, purple and scarlet fabric pomegranates (*Rimonim*), symbolizing thunder and lightning, respectively. He also wears the breastplate of Aaron, which has inset in it twelve precious gemstones in four rows of three stones each, with the names of the twelve tribes of Israel inscribed upon them. Joseph knew that in ancient times, the High Priest could interpret God's will from the scroll containing the divine 72 letter name of God, which was folded within the breastplate (the *Urim ve' Thumim*: the "Perfect Light"[118]) and which caused the names of the tribes on the stones in the breastplate to reveal hidden "tongues of fire" in answer to the question asked[119].

At the Nicanor Gate, the "footstool of God" referred to in Psalm 133, Mary and Joseph look out past the open-air sacrificial stone altar. To the left behind the altar is the *Kiyor*, the large metal water-storage vessel with twelve spigots starting at the bottom and ascending in a spiral around the Kiyor, which the Priests use to wash their hands and feet before the service. Each night, Joseph knew, the Kiyor was lowered by a pulley into a pool of water underneath the Temple so that the water inside the Kiyor would retain its character as "living water"[120]. Near the Kiyor are two tables, one of silver and one of marble to hold, respectively, the silver and gold vessels needed by the Priests for the service and to hold the fats of the animal sacrifices before the Priests offer them up on the altar.[121] Directly behind the northern side of the altar lies the entrance to the Sanctuary. Just inside it is the golden altar, which like the stone altar has four horns protruding from its corners, where the incense is burned and behind it, the two overlapping curtains shielding the Holy of Holies.

Mary and Joseph advance to the low stone parapet and tell the priest that they wish to give up two turtledoves as Mary's burnt offering and sin offering. The Court of the Priests is elevated by three steps (a total of 2 and ½ cubits high) from the Court of Israel, so the Priest must bend down to take the basket from Joseph and Mary. The Priest then lifts up the basket holding the two turtledoves and announces it to all assembled at the Nicanor Gate, saying *"Let this be recorded and remembered!"* [122]

The priest takes the turtledoves and sacrifices them, using a sharp fingernail on his right hand rather than a knife, smearing the blood of the birds on the southwestern corner of the stone altar, below the red line painted halfway up the side of the altar[123]. Joseph knows that the blood of animal sacrifices (other than bird sacrifices) are splashed on the altar above the red line, while wine and other non-living sacrificial offerings are splashed below the red line. Joseph glances over to his right and sees that at the middlemost of the northern gates, the Gate of Sacrifice, an Israelite has brought a lamb to be sacrificed as a sin-offering. The Israelite places his hands on the head of the lamb, confessing and placing his sins on the sacrificial lamb. A Priest then ties the head of the lamb to one of the 24 rings fastened in the ground to the north of the altar, preparing it for sacrifice. Joseph knows that in the morning the lambs are slaughtered after being tied to the second row of the northwestern rings, while in the late afternoon service, they are slaughtered after being tied to the second row of the northeastern set of rings, so that the sun clearly illuminates the area where the Priests are working and the shadow cast by the high stone altar does not interfere with the light.[124]

At this time, the eastern rings fastened in the stone floor to Joseph's right are in shadow, since the sun is low in the east, with only the western portion of the Azarah, the Courtyard of the Priests, being bathed in light. Other Priests are flaying bullocks being offered as private offerings on eight dwarf pillars to the north of the stone altar, on top of which pillars are cedar blocks with iron hooks for holding the sacrifices[125]. Other sacrifices are being flayed on marble tables to the north of the rings, with the Priests separating out those portions of fat and meat which will be salted and then burned on the altar. A portion of the balance of the meat from the sacrifices will be eaten by the Priests and their families[126].

Joseph looks up at the immense stone altar where the Priests, with heavily muscled arms, are throwing fats from the animal sacrifices onto one of the offertory fires from one side of the altar. The 1,500 ton altar stands 22½ feet high, 75 feet long and 75 feet wide, with the four corners of the altar jutting up like horns[127]. A gentle slope leads up from the south to the top of the altar and one Priest has advanced up the slope and is walking on a narrow ledge bordering the altar in a counterclockwise direction, entering from the right[128]. Joseph remembers that the altar was carved and constructed entirely without the use of iron[129], for it was believed that iron was created to shorten man's life, while the altar was created to lengthen his days. Joseph is amazed as always to see Priests standing on the top of the altar with bare feet, seemingly oblivious to the hot surface of the altar, kept hot by the sacrificial fires, which are kept continually burning. Joseph knows, however, that since the Courtyard of the Priests is holy, consecrated ground, the Priests are not allowed to wear shoes or sandals of any kind when walking in that area.

Joseph understands that just to the west of the Gate of Sacrifice (blocked from his view by the Sanctuary building) lies the Spark Gate, where a small fire is kept burning in case the altar fire ever went out[130]. Immediately to the right of the Gate of Sacrifice lies the Chamber of the Hearth, which contains four smaller chambers, one for inspection of lambs to be sacrificed, one for baking the Shewbread, a third for storage of an older altar which had been defiled and broken, and a final chamber where the Priests sleep at night and which leads to an underground mikveh used by the Priests. To the east of the Chamber of the Hearth is the Chamber of Hewn Stone which houses the "Parhedrin" or "Grand Sanhedrin", a Supreme Court of 71 judges[131]. A Chamber of Council adjoining the Parhedrin houses the High Priest during the seven days preceding Yom Kippur in a second story apartment, with the Chamber of Abtinus (the maker of the offering incense for the golden altar) on the first floor. Also adjoining the Parhedrin is the Chamber of the Pitcher, from which water is supplied to the Temple.

Joseph looks to his left toward the three southern gates, the Water Gate (with the High Priest's mikveh above it), the Gate of the Firstborn and the Gate of the Firewood. Joseph remembers also that a number of chambers to the south side of the Courtyard of Priests were used for special Temple functions: the Chamber of the Garment Maker (where the Priests' garments were made and stored), the Chamber of the Pan (where the High Priest's pan offering was prepared), the Chamber of Hides (with another mikveh for the High Priest above it) and finally the Rinsing Chamber and the Salt Chamber (for cleaning and salting the animal sacrifices). Joseph knew that in all there were eight chambers in the Courtyard of the Israelites, with the remaining chambers set along the side walls of the Courtyard of the Priests.[132] Although he has never seen it, Joseph has been told that the knives used by the Priests for slaughtering are kept in wall cubicles just inside the Entrance Hall of the Sanctuary.

Joseph puts aside his ruminations about the Temple chambers as the priest returns to sprinkle Mary with the balance of the sacrificial blood from the turtledoves and declare her cleansed and ritually pure. Jesus, as the firstborn, is then presented to the priest for redemption against payment of the five silver coins, as required under the Torah. The priest offers two benedictions for Jesus, one for the happy event which has given the family a firstborn and a second benediction for the law of redemption itself[133]. Joseph and Mary turn and walk down the fifteen steps to the Women's Courtyard where Simeon has stayed after the morning services in order to watch the private sacrifices and purifications.

XIV
(Psalm 133)

"Behold, how good and how pleasant it is
for brethren to dwell together in unity!
It is like the precious ointment
upon the head, even Aaron's beard:
that went down over the hem of his garments ...."

As the priest sprinkles the sacrificial blood on Mary and blesses Jesus, **imagine that Simeon looks up and sees the red cloth ribbon which Mary had tied to the outside of the basket holding Jesus turn from red to white**. Simeon immediately recognizes this as the sign he sought from God that his dream was a true vision. Simeon had for many years attended the ceremony on the Day of Atonement (Yom Kippur) when two goats have red cloth ribbons tied to them and one goat is sacrificed on the altar to atone for Priests who had entered the Temple or eaten sacrifices while ritually impure[134]. The other goat (the scapegoat) is taken by a non-Israelite into the wilderness to be thrown down from a high cliff [*la-Azazel*], offered as a sacrifice in atonement for all the people's sins, other than the sins atoned for by the first goat offered up in sacrifice to the Lord[135].

When Simeon was a child, it had been the custom for the Priests to tie a piece of the red cloth ribbon from the goat led out to the wilderness to the porch of the Sanctuary building. If after the goat was taken out into the wilderness, the red cloth ribbon tied to the Sanctuary building turned from red to white, it signified to the people that God's forgiveness had been granted, as it is written in Isaiah 1:18: "Come now, and let us reason together, saith the Lord: though your sins be as scarlet, they shall be as white as snow; though they be red like crimson, they shall be as wool" [136]. As Simeon grew older, during some of the Yom Kippur festivals the red cloth had failed to turn white, to the great distress of the people, so the Priests in recent years had taken to having the red cloth tied to the cliff where the goat was sacrificed rather than on the Porch of Solomon[137].

When the red cloth ribbon tied to the basket holding Jesus turned white, Simeon recognizes the Day of Atonement sign from his youth. Simeon instantly knows that he has just seen the sign that Jesus was the one chosen to be sent out as a revelation to the Gentiles and to the glory of Israel. Simeon rushes up the Mary and Joseph to embrace them and the child, Jesus. The sign of the red cloth ribbon turning white as a sign to Simeon is evoked in Hebrews 13:11-13, where it is written: "For the bodies of those animals whose blood is brought into the sanctuary by the high priest as a sacrifice for sin are burned outside the camp [*red heifer and goat on Yom Kippur*]. So Jesus suffered outside the gate in order to sanctify the people through his own blood." It is also written in Leviticus 17:11: "...for it is the blood that maketh an atonement for the soul." [Sinai Tanakh].

XV
(Psalm 134)

"Behold, bless ye the Lord, all ye servants of the Lord,
which by night stand in the house of the Lord.
Lift up your hands in the sanctuary, and bless the Lord.
The Lord that made heaven and earth
bless thee out of Zion."

Leaving the Women's Courtyard, Mary and Joseph exit the Temple area with their child Jesus and enter the Courtyard of the Gentiles on the way out of the Temple area, returning to their room at the inn, wondering to themselves why Simeon was moved to tell them that Jesus would be a light for revelation to the Gentiles for the glory of the people of Israel.

Postscript

The Temple High Priest traditionally celebrated the last day of the Feast of Tabernacles (Sukkot), by pouring "living" water from the Pool of Siloam out of a golden pitcher onto the stone altar[138]. The High Priest's offering of water was in fulfillment of Isaiah 12:3 [Sinai Tanakh], "Therefore with joy shall ye draw water out of the wells of salvation". It was during the seven days of the Sukkot festival that the Temple Priests would also sacrifice 70 bullocks to atone for the sins of the seventy nations of the world, with the number of bulls sacrificed being diminished each day to reflect the diminishment of the Gentile nations over time[139], and then on the eighth day sacrifice one last bullock for Israel itself - the one-day festival of Shemini Atzeret[140]. During Sukkot, the Priests would also lead the worshippers in a processional seven times around the stone altar, with the worshippers beating the ground with willow branches while Levites played flutes. The worshippers would also sing the Great Hosanna [*Hosanna* meaning "Save I pray"] on the seventh day -the day known as Hosanna Rabbah.[141] After the destruction of the Second Temple by the Romans in 70 C.E., Rabbinic Judaism created the concept of the Jewish home as a family sanctuary (with family celebrations of the Shabbat, Sukkot, Pesach and Chanukah) and instituted prayers in Synagogue services to replace the Temple sacrificial services[142]. Rabbinic Judaism also stressed salvation for Jews who believed in the written and oral law of the Torah - the figurative "water out of the wells of salvation", rather than the literal waters from the Pool of Siloam.

With the destruction of the Second Temple, the sacrifices by the Temple Priests of the seventy bullocks during the Sukkot services on behalf of the Gentiles ceased and the sins of the Gentiles could have gone unatoned. However, since the Gentile nations were not being diminished in number by being brought to the God of Israel through conversion to Judaism (as reflected in the ritual's decreasing number of bulls sacrificed each of the seven days of Sukkot), Gentiles were brought to the God of Abraham through belief in Jesus. Jesus had once stood in the Basilica in the Royal Porch where the shops and Treasury resided, on the last day of the Festival of Sukkot. Speaking with prophetic foreknowledge of the Temple's coming destruction[143], Jesus had said to the assembled multitude: *"If any man thirst, let him come unto me, and drink. He who believes in me, as the scripture said, 'Out of his heart shall flow rivers of living water'"* (John 7:37- 38). Although Jesus' statement probably sounded to devout Jews at the time as if he were usurping Temple ritual, Jesus' call to the Gentiles to join the faithful and drink of the figurative "wells of salvation" prefigured a similar call by Rabbis to Jews after the Temple's destruction, in fulfillment of Hosea 14:3 "We will render, instead of bulls, [the offering of prayers by] our lips"[144]. The next two segments of this book, *"Sign of Jonah"* and *"Dominion"* will attempt to show that the belief Jesus called for was not the creation of a second Godhead, but rather a call to Gentiles to repent and believe in the one God of Israel.

Finally, it should be noted that Simeon as portrayed in Luke 2:29-32 does not characterize Jesus as a revelation to Gentiles and Jews, **but to Gentiles alone**, and yet his life is described as being to **the glory of God's people Israel**. As the sacrifice of the Yom Kippur goat of Azazel atoned for the sins of the people of Israel, turning the red cloth ribbon tied to the temple porch white, so Jesus' perfect sacrifice of himself atoned for the sins of the Gentiles. As it is written in Isaiah 1:18: "Come now, and let us reason together, saith the Lord: though your sins be as scarlet, they shall be as white as snow; though they be red like crimson, they shall be as wool"

This is consistent with the thesis of this book that Jesus brings Gentiles to the faith of

Abraham as a wild olive branch to be grafted onto the olive tree of Israel, with both Jews and Christians representing two religions bound by one faith to God. The destruction of the Second Temple can therefore be seen as a pivotal point in the creation of rabbinic Judaism and Christianity as two daughter religions. Both evolved out of Temple Judaism and due in part to the destruction of the Second Temple, the followers of both religions were dispersed throughout the world to act as witnesses to the God of Israel. For even though the Second Temple has been destroyed, the Presence of God can be found with those who bear witness to His name in the world.

As Rabbi Hillel the Elder used to recite during the rejoicing at the Pool of Siloam during the Feast of Tabernacles:

"When I am here, everyone is here; but when I am not here who is here? To the place that I love, there my feet lead me.' The Holy One's response: '*In every place where I cause my Name to be mentioned, I will come to thee and bless thee*' (Exod. 20:21). [emphasis added]"[145]

This echoes Matthew 18:20:

"*For where two or three are gathered in my name, there am I in the midst of them*." [emphasis added]

As a result of this, although the Temple Priests no longer can lift up their hands to bless God in His Sanctuary [the Second Temple], the God of Israel has truly blessed the world "out of Zion", as is written in Psalm 134.

"Psalm 150"

Psalm 150, the Psalm of David, is celebrated in a French
hymn from 1568. The gold center panel contains Hebrew
calligraphy from the Psalms. Collage mixed media 1996
11" x 8.5" - Sandra Bowden

SIGN OF JONAH

"The Storm on the Sea of Galilee, after Rembrandt"

The Storm on the Sea of Galilee is a painting from 1633 by the Dutch Golden Age painter Rembrandt van Rijn. The painting depicts the miracle of Jesus calming the storm on the Sea of Galilee, as depicted in the fourth chapter of the Gospel of Mark in the New Testament. It is Rembrandt's only seascape. Mixed media with gold leaf 2014 8" x 6" – Sandra Bowden

SIGN OF JONAH

"When the crowds were increasing, he [Jesus] began to say:
'This generation is an evil generation[146]:
it seeks a sign[147], but no sign shall be given it
except the sign of Jonah.
For as Jonah became a sign to the men of Nineveh,
so will the Son of man be to this generation'. "

- Luke 11:29

Each of the four gospels (Matthew, Mark, Luke and John) include descriptions of Jesus citing to the sign of Jonah[148]. The popular interpretation of these passages is that Jesus is indicating that just as Jonah emerged from the belly of the great fish after three days, so Jesus would rise again from the dead after three days. Luke appears to emphasize instead Jesus' role as a preacher or missionary fulfilling the mission of Jonah[149]. These two interpretations of the sign of Jonah are both critical to understanding Jesus, but I will start with the latter interpretation, since I believe the life, death and resurrection of Jesus can only be truly understood if viewed in the context of Jesus' role as God's missionary to the Gentiles.

Jonah was a devout Jew who resisted God's command to go to Nineveh, a city of Gentile sinners, and warn them to repent. The Jewish Sages commented on Jonah 1:3 [Sinai Tanakh] ("But Jonah rose up to flee unto Tarshish from the presence of the Lord"), saying:

> *"Why did Jonah flee? Because when ... the Holy One sent him ... to Jerusalem to announce that He would destroy it [and] Israel resolved to repent, the Holy One, in the abundance of His mercy, regretted the evil decree and did not destroy Jerusalem. Hence Israel called Jonah 'a lying prophet'... [when] the Holy One sent him against Nineveh, Jonah reasoned with himself: I know that this people are prone to repentance, and so they are likely to repent... It is not enough that Israel call me 'a lying prophet'? Shall the nations of the world do likewise? I have no choice but to flee."[150].*

The Jewish Sages thus recognize that Jonah did not wish to save the Gentiles and bring them under God's grace if that meant further damage to his own reputation.

Jesus as God's Missionary to the Gentiles

The significance of the story of Jonah as the sign of Jesus is that Jesus, unlike Jonah, was willing to suffer even death in order to do God's will and bring salvation to the Gentiles. That

Jesus viewed himself as God's messenger of repentance and forgiveness to the Gentile nations is clear from the following two passages:

> *"Then he [Jesus] opened their minds to understand the scriptures, and said to them, 'Thus it is written, that the Christ should suffer and on the third day rise from the dead, and that repentance and forgiveness of sins should be preached in his name **to all nations, beginning from Jerusalem** [emphasis added]"*: Luke 24:44-47

and

> *"It was the feast of the Dedication at Jerusalem [**Chanukah**]; it was winter, and Jesus was walking in the temple, in the portico of Solomon. So the Jews gathered round him and said to him, 'How long will you keep us in suspense? If you are the Christ, tell us plainly.' Jesus answered them, 'I told you, and you do not believe. The works that I do in my Father's name, they bear witness to me; but you do not believe, because **you do not belong to my sheep**. My sheep hear my voice, and I know them, and they follow me; and I give them eternal life...."* [emphasis and explanatory text added]: John 10:22-28

Just as Jonah was God's messenger of repentance and forgiveness to the Gentiles of Nineveh, Jesus was God's messenger of repentance and forgiveness to the Gentiles of the world. God-fearing Jews fully honoring the Torah were not viewed by Jesus as belonging to his flock of sheep, but rather tax collectors and other "sinners" -that is, Israelites who had succumbed to the secular world - and thereafter, the Gentiles. As it is written in 1 Timothy 1:15: "This is a true saying, and worthy of all men to be received, that Christ Jesus came into the world to save sinners." And as is written in Matthew 9:11-13:

> *"And when the Pharisees saw this, they said to his disciples, 'Why does your teacher eat with tax collectors and sinners?' But when he heard it, he said, 'Those who are well have no need of a physician, but those who are sick. Go and learn what this means, 'I desire mercy, not sacrifice,' **For I came not to call the righteous, but sinners**.'[emphasis added]"*

Devout Jews as the First Disciples of Jesus:
Judaism has Ongoing Validity and
"Salvation is from the Jews"

Although Jesus preached primarily in Jewish communities[151] and instructed his early disciples to do likewise, this may have been because Jesus wished to develop a cadre of Jewish disciples, so that the Gentile nations those disciples later would bring to God would acknowledge that "salvation is from the Jews" (John 4:22). Equally clear is that Jesus did not view his mission on earth as involving the denial or voiding of the covenant of God with Israel or the validity of the Torah. As Jesus said:

> *"Think not that I have come to abolish the law and the prophets; I have come not to abolish them but to fulfill them. For truly, I say to you, **til heaven and earth pass away not an iota, not a dot, will pass from the law** until all is accomplished": Matthew 5:17-18 [emphasis added]*

Jesus also makes this position clear in his parables ("*Mashal*" in Hebrew). As Jesus explains in the **parable of the prodigal son**, the younger son *[the Gentile]* has squandered his inheritance in loose living, but then repents and returns home, and is forgiven by the father *[God]*. The father reassures the older brother *[the Israelite]* who stayed at home with the father and dutifully served him, saying: "Son you are always with me, and all that is mine is yours. It was fitting to make merry and be glad, for this your brother was dead, and he is alive, he was lost, and is found." (Luke 15:31-32). This principle is even more clearly expressed in Matthew 20:1-16, where the **Kingdom of Heaven is likened to a householder who hires laborers for his vineyard** and pays those coming in the eleventh hour to work in the vineyard *[the Gentiles saved through Jesus]* the same amount as those laborers who had worked the entire day in the vineyard *[the devout Jews honoring the covenant of the Torah]* - both devout Christian and devout Jew receive the same "wages": entrance to the Kingdom of Heaven.

Certainly, Jesus did not appear to view the Temple as lacking religious validity. At the age of twelve, Jesus stays behind after Passover celebrations to sit in the Temple and listen to, and question, the elders and tells his parents that the Temple is his "Father's house" (see Luke 2:41-49). Later, during his ministry, Jesus cures a leper and then tells him:

> *"See that you say nothing to anyone; but go, show yourself to the priest [so the priest can determine that the Tzara'as (divine leprosy) is gone], and offer for your cleansing what Moses commanded [i.e., go to the Chamber of the Lepers in the Temple and make the ritual offering for purification]." (Mark 1:44)[explanatory text added].*

Rather, Jesus appears to want the Temple's sanctity to be expanded. Jesus chases the moneylenders out of the Temple Mount area, saying to them "Is it not written, 'My house shall be called a house of prayer *for all the nations*? [emphasis added]' but you have made it into a den of robbers." (Mark 11:17-18; Luke 19:45-47). It is important to note that the moneylenders (exchanging shekels for pagan money) and the traders selling lambs and doves for sacrifice had their booths outside the main Temple, either in the area of shops near the Huldah Gates, or in the basilica comprising the Royal Porch, which did not even open onto the Courtyard of Gentiles[152] and which was traditionally not viewed as being part of the Temple[153]. Thus, Jesus is shown as viewing not only the portion of the Temple Mount reserved for Jews as holy, but also the public portion open to Gentiles. This is consonant with the thesis of this book that Jesus was to be a light for revelation to the Gentiles. The apostles also did not view Jesus as nullifying the Torah and the validity of Temple Judaism. As Luke 24:53 makes clear, after seeing the risen Christ, the apostles "returned to Jerusalem with great joy, and were continually *in the temple* blessing God." [emphasis added]

Christians should also try to picture in their mind not the popular cultural image of Jesus wearing a unadorned, plain robe, but rather **picture Jesus as wearing a *Tallit* and *Tefillin* as all observant Jews did in his time**[154]. The **Tallit** [now the modern-day prayer shawl], in the time of Jesus was a large rectangular cloth worn over the tunic and falling to the ankles. On the four corners of the Tallit were affixed tassels of eight threads (one of which was blue) with five double knots (with the fringes being called *tzitzit*), in keeping with Numbers 15:37-41. **Tefillin**, or phylacteries, were not the leather boxes currently worn by observant Jews, but in the time of Jesus were flat leather pouches resembling kerchiefs which are tied to the arm and forehead and worn during weekday morning services. The Tefillin contained passages from the Torah, including the Shema, in fulfillment of Deuteronomy 6:8: "bind them for a sign upon your hand and for frontlets between your eyes"[155]. That Jesus wore Tallit and Tefillin can be inferred from his criticism, recounted in Matthew 23:5, of those Jews who wore extra-long Tzitzit on their Tallit and wore extra-wide Tefillin as an extra show of piety, rather than just wear prayer shawl fringes and Tefillin of normal size, as was the tradition.[156] Also, as recorded in Matthew 9:20-21, a woman suffering from an issue of blood touches the woolen tassels (*kraspedon* in the Greek) of the hem of Jesus' garment - the Tzitzit of his Tallit - and is healed[157]. And it is noteworthy that the Jewish followers of Jesus apparently did not abandon the practice of wearing Tefillin even after Jesus' death. As A. Kolatch has noted:

> *"It is interesting that the Talmud forbids one to paint boxes of tefillin with gold paint in order to make them conspicuous because this was the practice of the minim. Minim, often translated as 'sectaries', is the name used in the Talmud for Christians. It appears from this reference that **for quite a few centuries after the beginning of Christianity, Christians continued to observe the Jewish law pertaining to the wearing of tefillin**. [emphasis added]"*[158]

Finally, despite Jesus' de-emphasizing the Jewish dietary rules for his disciples, it is clear that they were followed by Jesus himself (see Mark 7:1-5, where the Pharisees do not state that Jesus is violating the Mosaic dietary laws, but merely some of his disciples) and were still largely followed by some of his disciples even after Jesus' death. For example, long after the death and resurrection of Jesus, Peter has a dream where he is urged by a voice from heaven to eat all manners of creatures, Peter says "No, Lord; for I have never eaten anything that is common or unclean" (Acts 10:14)[159]

Bringing Gentiles to the One God of Israel

Jesus also made it clear that his role was to bring believers **to the one God**, not to create a second Godhead:

> "And Jesus cried out and said, 'He who believes in me, believes **not in me but in him who sent me**. And he who sees me sees him who sent me. I have come as light into the world, that whoever believes in me may not remain in darkness.": John 12:44-46 [emphasis added]

And as Irving Zeitlin has noted[160], describing Jesus' reading of Isaiah 61 in the synagogue:

> "By the juxtaposition of the acts of Elijah and Elisha and Isaiah 61, Jesus implies 'that the words meaning poor, captive, blind and oppressed do not apply exclusively to any in-group but, on the contrary, apply to those whom God wishes them to apply. God sent Elijah and Elisha to outsiders, the Sidonian widow and the Syrian leper.' What Jesus' fellow villagers found offensive, then, was not only that he had arrogated to himself this passage of unique prophetic authority, but that he also declared that **the aphesis (redemption) of which it speaks will include in the End Time, those outside Israel."** [emphasis added]

Various passages in the New Testament amplify the concept that Jesus should be understood as an aspect of God's presence in this world, not as a separate Godhead. For example, Jesus is likened to God's gift of **manna in the wilderness**:

> "Jesus said to them, 'I am the bread of life; he who comes to me shall not hunger, and he who believes in me shall never thirst...For I have come down from heaven, not to do my own will, but the will of him who sent me...Your fathers ate the manna in the wilderness, and they died...I am the living bread which came down from heaven....": John 6:35-38

or God's gift of **water from the rock** which traveled with Israel in the wilderness:

> "I want you to know, brethren, that our fathers were all under the cloud, and all passed through the sea, and all were baptized into Moses in the cloud and in the sea, and all ate the same supernatural drink. For they drank from the supernatural Rock which followed

them, and the Rock was Christ": I Corinthians 10:1-5

or, finally, as the **serpent on Moses' staff** which healed any of the Israelites in the wilderness bitten by a serpent (Numbers 21:89):

"And as Moses lifted up the serpent in the wilderness, so must the Son of man be lifted up, that whoever believes in him may have eternal life.": John 3:14-15

Just as God provided manna, water from the rock and the healing serpent to sustain the Israelites in their wanderings through the wilderness, Jesus was sent to the Gentiles of the nations in their spiritual wilderness. The above passages picture Jesus as akin to God's supernatural gifts of manna, water and healing to Israel in the desert, flowing directly from God, but ***not creating separate Godheads.***

Jesus Teaches the *Shema*, The Jewish
Declaration of Faith in One God

Indeed, as Mark 12:28-29 recounts, when Jesus is asked by a scribe which commandment is first of all, Jesus answers by reciting Deuteronomy 6:4-5, the first two passages of the "***Shema***" (so-named because the first word of the passage - "Hear, O Israel" - is "*Shema*" in Hebrew):

"Jesus answered, 'The first is, "Hear, O Israel: The Lord our God, the Lord is one; and you shall love the Lord your God with all your heart and with all your soul, and with all your mind, and with all your strength."

To make clear the significance of Jesus quoting the first two passages of the Shema, it should be noted that the Shema is the ultimate Jewish declaration of faith in the one God and is the first prayer Jewish children are taught and traditionally is the last utterance on the deathbed. The Shema was read as part of the Temple service by the priests following the daily morning offering, with the people responding "Blessed is the name of His Glorious Majesty forever and ever." On Yom Kippur (the Day of Atonement), the Shema marks the conclusion of the day. Rabbi Judah Ha-Nasi, the compiler of the Mishnah, believed that the Torah required Jews to recite the Shema above all other prayers[161]. By tradition in Judaism, the last letter of the first word of the Shema prayer, the *a'yin* in the word "Hear (*Shema*)", and the last letter of the last word of the Shema, the *dalet* in the word "one (*echad*)", are written by the scribe (sofer) in large script. The two letters, *a'yin* and *dalet*, spell "*ayd*", which means "witness", signifying that Israel is intended to serve as a witness in the world to the glory of the one God[162].

Jesus as the Light from the First Day of Creation:
Begotten of God, Not Made or Created
and of the Same Substance as God

Perhaps the use of midrashic commentaries could best present the religious significance of Jesus to the Gentiles. It is written in Genesis 1:3-4 [Sinai Tanakh], "And God said: Let there be light: and there was light. And God saw the light, that it was good: and God divided the light from the darkness". One Jewish Sage, Rabbi Eleazar said:

"By the light that the Holy One created on the first day, one could see from one end of the world to the other. But as soon as the Holy One observed the generation of the flood and the generation of the dispersion of mankind, and saw that their conduct was to be depraved, He proceeded to secrete His light from them. And for whom did He secrete it? For the righteous in the time-to-come, just like a king who has a goodly treasure and sets it aside for his son. And where did He hide the light? In the Garden of Eden [i.e., in the world to come]."[163] *[explanatory text added]*

Rashi's commentary on Genesis 1:4 confirms the above interpretation from the Aggadah:

"And God saw that the light was good and He separated....":

Rashi: Here too we need the words of the Aggadah: He saw that the wicked were unworthy of using it; He therefore set it apart for the righteous in the world to come."[164]

Rashi's "Drash" is extremely perceptive, since a comparison of Genesis 1:1-4 (first day of creation) and Genesis 1:14-19(fourth day of creation) reveals that after God says "Let there be light" on the first day of creation, God separated the light from the darkness. Then on the fourth day of creation, God "made" the lights of the firmament (stars, sun and moon) to provide light for the earth and to divide night from day. The light of the first day of creation was not used, since it had been set aside for the world to come ("*olam haba*"). It is important to recognize as well that when the "Ruach HaKodesh", the "wind" (i.e., the "breath" or "spirit") of God moved upon the face of the waters, ***the light was begotten solely with His Word***: "Let there be light..." (see Genesis 1:3 [Sinai Tanakh]). By way of contrast, God "***made***" the firmament dividing the waters above (heaven) from the waters below (earth and seas) (second day) (see Genesis 1:7), "***made***" the sun, moon and stars (fourth day) (Genesis 1:16), "***created*** great whales, and every living creature ..." (fifth day) (Genesis 1:21), and "***made** the beasts of the earth*" (Genesis 1:25) and "***created*** man in His own image" (sixth day") (Genesis 1:27). It has also been noted by Jewish scholars that the word for the light of the fourth day is spelled defectively, missing the letter "*vav*", indicating that "the light emanating from celestial bodies is not equal to the richness and purity of the primeval light [of the first day of creation]"[165].

In one sense, Jesus may be God's light, set aside at the time of creation, but later become flesh through the Word of God, and placed on earth as a "*light* for revelation to the Gentiles [emphasis added]" (see Luke 2:29-34). As it is written:

"***In the beginning was the Word***, *and the Word was with God, and the Word was God... In him was life, and the life was the light of men. **The light shines in the darkness***, *and the darkness has not overcome it ... And the Word became flesh and dwelt among us, full of grace and truth; we have beheld his glory....[emphasis added]": John 1:14*

and

"*For God so loved the world that he gave his only Son, that whoever believes in him should not perish but have eternal life... And this is the judgment, that **the light has come into the world***, *and ... he who does what is true comes to the light, that it may be clearly seen that his deeds have been wrought in God.[emphasis added]": John 3:16-21*

And as the "*Quicunque Vult*", the Creed of Saint Athanasius (part of the original Catholic liturgy for Trinity Sunday) formulated Church doctrine on the Holy Trinity for Christians:

"*The Father is made of none, neither created, nor begotten.*
The Son is of the Father alone, not made, nor created, **but begotten***.*
The Holy Ghost is of the Father and the Son, neither made, nor created, nor begotten, **but proceeding***. [emphasis added]"*[166]

That the light begotten on the first day, the light set aside and reserved for the world to come, is **of the same substance as God** may be seen from Isaiah 60:19, where it is written that in the world to come:

"*The sun shall no more be thy light by day; neither for brightness shall the moon give light unto thee: but **the Lord shall be unto thee an everlasting light***, *and thy God thy glory.[emphasis added]"*

Psalm 104, which is recited in synagogues beginning with the Sabbath on which the Torah portion of Bereishit [Genesis] is read, until the holiday of Pesach [Passover], is recited at that time because it is believed to recount the entire creation, starting with the first day, where God's glory is seen as a garment of light:

"**Cloaked in light** *as a garment, Who stretches out the heavens like a curtain, Who roofs His upper chambers with water (v. 2,3)[emphasis added]"*[167].

The concept of God's light appearing on earth to reveal His will is not unique to Christianity. Rashi, commenting on Exodus 2:2 [Sinai Tanakh], where the mother of Moses sees at his birth "that he was a goodly child", interprets this to mean that when Moses was born the whole house became filled with supernatural light, since the same phrasing is used as when God sees the light of the first day of creation is good[168]. That same primal light shone again from Moses's face when he came down from Mount Sinai:

> *"That Light **returned** to Moshe when he stood on Mount Sinai and he was able to perceive through it for the rest of his life. The intensity of this Light is why the people were unable to get close to him unless he masked his face.*"[169] *[emphasis added]*

Harmonization of the Trinity with the Belief in One God

Many Christians traditionally affirm their beliefs by reciting the Nicene Creed during Church services:

> *"We believe in One God,*
> *the Father, the Almighty,*
> *maker of heaven and earth,*
> *of all that is, seen and unseen.*
> *We believe in one Lord, Jesus Christ,*
> *the only Son of God,*
> *eternally begotten of the Father,*
> *God from God, **Light from Light**,*
> *true God from true God,*
> *begotten, not made,*
> *of one Being with the Father...*
> *[emphasis added]*"[170]

As formulated by the Council of Nicea (325 A.D.) under the theory of "*homoousios*", Christians are monotheists, believing in one God, but also believing that God's light took the form of a flesh and blood man on earth - Jesus - to urge repentance and offer salvation. God's Word sustained the Israelites by producing manna from heaven and water from a rock in the desert and taking the form of light radiating around Moses in order to inspire his mother to extra efforts to save Moses from Pharaoh's decree of death. Is it not also possible that God's Word (the light set aside from the first day of creation) could have been made flesh as a man in order to act as a "***light for revelation*** to the Gentiles and to the glory of thy people Israel [emphasis added]?"

For is it not written in the Letter of Paul to the Colossians 1:15-19 that Jesus is "the first-born of all creation" - the light of God begotten on the first day? That the light was begotten first of all things is supported by the Jewish Sages: "R. Judah taught: The light was created first, and then [all that is in] the world."[171].

Further, although John's evocation of Jesus as the Word ["*logos*"] of God has Hellenistic overtones to it, the underlying Hebrew meaning of the "word" has not been abandoned and is still prominently evoked in the text:

> *"When, therefore, the Fourth Evangelist [John] pronounces the word logos at the beginning of his Gospel, the many different profound meanings of dabhar ["word" in Hebrew] as well as of logos ["word" in Greek] harmonize into a beautiful and mysterious unity for him as well as for his Greek-speaking readers familiar with the Old Testament in the same way as the sound of several church bells run simultaneously. Duerr and the many New Testament exegetes of the same opinion may be right in their view that the Old Testament tone is strongest...."[172].*

Jesus Being Fully Divine and Fully Human
Not Necessarily a Violation of the Torah

One of the other major focal points of difficulty between Jews and Christians is the issue of Jesus being a human with divine origins. Part of this difficulty may be the religious doctrine within Judaism that God's creations are not meant to be mixed so as to create hybrids. Thus, the tractate of the Talmud called *Kilayim* deals with forbidden mixtures, such as "*Shaatnez*", the mixing of linen and wool in clothing. As one Jewish commentator noted:

> *"In support of the theory that fear of the hybrid as representing disorder lay at the basis of some dietary laws, one could cite the biblical prohibition on other mixed species (in Hebrew, kilayim): Jews were forbidden to sow together two kinds of grain, to graft two plant species, to crossbreed two kinds of animals, to plow with an ox and an ass together, and to mix wool and linen in the same cloth. This was also perhaps one of the reasons the Jews rejected Jesus: Christ, the man-God, was the absolute hybrid creature, and therefore unthinkable[173].*

This prohibition of *Kilayim* is akin to the proscription against making graven images. There are exceptions, however, to the *shaatnez* rule and the graven image prohibition, if specifically ordained by God. Thus, the priest's girdle not used on Yom Kippur may contain both linen and wool threads[174] and a linen garment bearing "*tzitzis*" (prayer shawl fringes) may use wool thread for the fringes[175]. Similarly, even though graven images are forbidden, the mercy seat of the ark bore the golden images of two cherubim, which were exempt from the prohibition because specifically ordained by God. Christians believe that Jesus had both a divine and human nature (e.g., both fully divine and fully human, as set forth by the Council of Chalcedon (451 A.D.)[176]. However, since Christians believe that this was ordained by God to serve His will, then it arguably would not violate the principles of *Kilayim* (forbidden mixtures), if true.

The Holy Spirit

It is important to recognize as well that the "Spirit of God", which moved over the waters in Genesis 1:1, is identified by Christians as the Holy Ghost or Holy Spirit. For example, the "Thanksgiving over the Water" for the rite of baptism reads: "We thank you Almighty God, for the gift of water. Over it the Holy Spirit moved in the beginning of creation."[177]. What Christians call the Holy Spirit is known to Jews as the "*Ruach HaKodesh*" or the "wind" (i.e., the "breath" or "spirit") of God that hovered over the waters of creation in Genesis 1:1 and the breath of God that parted the waters of the Red Sea (Exodus 14:21). God also formed man from the dust by breathing into his nostrils the breath of life (Genesis 2:7).

First century Christians, many of whom were devout Jews, also identified the Holy Spirit in terms similar to the spirit or breath of God (see, e.g., John 3:8: "The Spirit blows where it wills..."). At Pentecost, the Holy Spirit descended on the apostles: "And suddenly a sound came from heaven like the rush of a mighty wind and it filled all the house where they were sitting ... And they were all filled with the Holy Spirit and began to speak in other tongues, as the Spirit gave them utterance." (Acts 2:2-4).

The critical point is that the Christian concept of the Trinity, if viewed against Jewish beliefs, may roughly equate Jesus to the Jewish Midrashic light from the first day of creation which was begotten, but not made or created - the glory of God which is the light of the world to come. The Christian Holy Spirit may be roughly equated to the Jewish "*Ruach HaKodesh*" or "breath" of God. The theological concept of the Holy Trinity of "Father, Son and Holy Ghost" evolved from these rough equivalencies. For example, the concept of the Holy Ghost later takes on a personal aspect, since it "bears witness", "cries", and "is grieved" (Romans 8:16; Galatians 4:6; Ephesians 4:30)[178]. Nevertheless, the initial origins of Jesus as the Jewish Midrashic light from the first day of creation and the Holy Spirit as the Jewish "Ruach HaKodesh" can still be seen as clearly rooted in Judaism. The cores of the Jewish and Christian theologies with respect to the One God therefore may not be as radically divergent from each other as it first appears or as is popularly thought.

Jesus' Healing as Teaching About
The Resurrection in the World to Come

Aside from telling parables about the world to come, Jesus spent a significant amount of time urging all to repent (see Luke 13:5 "...unless you repent you will all likewise perish") and healing physical and spiritual ills and casting out demons. Jesus is seen in the Gospels healing numerous people, sometimes by his mere command and sometimes by the laying on of hands or other physical contact. Jesus is described as curing leprosy, blindness, a withered arm, deaf-muteness, paralysis, dropsy and lameness and as casting out demons from people[179].

The healing of the lepers is clearly the most important of all the healings and more important even than the casting out of demons. In the incident where Jesus cures the leper and tells him to go to the Temple Priest to perform the appropriate ritual (Mark 1:44), Jesus' instructions make it clear that the leper is suffering from *"Tzara'as"*, a spiritual leprosy, and not clinical leprosy. In clinical leprosy, the skin is swollen and darkens, while in *"Tzara'as"* the skin does not swell and the affected areas turn white.[180] Also, people suffering from *"Tzara'as"* were allowed to live within cities which were not walled, since it was not believed contagious.

The Jewish Sages believed that *"Tzara'as"* was caused by the commission of one of ten sins: (1) serving idols, (2) immorality, (3) murder, (4) desecration of the Name of Heaven, (5) blasphemy of the Almighty, (6) robbing the public, (7) acting in a capacity not permitted to the person, (8) conceit, (9) *"lashon hara"* or the evil tongue[181], or (10) taking a vain oath[182]. Normally, a Priest would examine the leper to determine if the condition had improved (i.e., the sinner had sufficiently repented). Again, the physical evidence of a cure did not match the cure for clinical leprosy - if the whiteness had spread over the entire body or the affected area had turned darker, the Priest would declare the condition cured and the person spiritually pure (*"tahor"*)[183].

Accordingly, since the ten sins which would result in *Tzara'as* were very great, it was believed that divine leprosy was inflicted by God Himself upon the sinner in order to prompt him to sincere repentance (*"Teshuvah"*)[184]. Although lepers were allowed to live within non-walled cities, they were required to grow their hair long and rend their garments as a sign of mourning and proclaim *"Tamay"* (impure) upon encountering anyone, lest they also touch him and become spiritually impure[185]. It was also believed that *Tzara'as* first was inflicted on the sinner's clothing (in the form of red or green spots) or the walls of his house, as a warning, before being inflicted on the sinner's skin. Since *Tzara'as* was believed to be caused by God Himself, the ability of Jesus to cure it at will would clearly have indicated to his followers that Jesus possessed divine powers. This power is noted in two passages. In one case of a woman healed of excessive bleeding, Jesus says that he felt "power" go out of him (Mark 5:30; Luke 8:46). On another occasion, Luke 6:19 records: "And all the crowd sought to touch him for power came forth from him and he healed them all." The Gospels note that Jesus *spoke* as one with divine authority (Matthew 7:28-29). The healing of the leper suffering from *Tzara'as* would have shown Jesus' followers that he also **acted** with divine authority.

The healing of the lepers and the other healing performed by Jesus, however, should not be seen as miracles used merely to convince his followers of his divine origin, because Jesus consistently refused to offer his followers signs of his divine mission other than the sign of Jonah. Instead, the healing should be seen as another example of Jesus teaching his followers. **The lesson of the healing is that since Jesus represented the power of the world to come, in the world to come the repentant believer in God would be resurrected, free of suffering and the evil impulse ("*yetzer hara*") and therefore free of all bodily and spiritual ills, including "*Tzara'as*".**

The healing of the lepers by Jesus can be seen as a **revelation in deeds** rather than in parables, intended for Gentiles unfamiliar with the Jewish belief in the resurrection of the body in the world to come, of the **nature of resurrection**. As Jesus said to one person he healed, "Your faith has healed you" (Mark 5:34; 10:52; Luke 7:50) and "... if I drive out demons by the finger of God, then the Kingdom of God has come to you." (Luke 11:20). That Jesus taught the truth of the resurrection of the body as believed by the Pharisees and scribes (precursors of Rabbinic Judaism) is clear, since Jesus is shown disputing with the Sadducees, who did not believe in the resurrection of the body. Jesus wins the approval of the Pharisees and scribes with his teaching that in the world to come men "cannot die anymore, because they are equal to angels and are sons of God, being sons of the resurrection" (Mark 12:18-28; Matthew 22:23-33; Luke 20:27-40).

Bringing the Gentiles to the God of Israel as a a Jewish Goal: Creating the Kingdom of God on Earth

The effect of growing closer to God is shown by how Noah, Abraham and Moses each reacted to God, when He threatened to punish sinners in the world. Noah said nothing in defense of others, but just started to build the ark. Abraham protested to God that the righteous should not perish with the wicked of Sodom. After the Israelites made the golden calf, prompting God's wrath, Moses begged God to spare all of the Israelites, and if not, to blot Moses out as well. The progression is from Noah who did not pray for his generation at all, to Abraham who prayed only for the righteous of his generation, to Moses who prayed for all of his generation, including the sinners, and was even prepared to share their fate[186]. I personally believe that Christians often go overboard in taking cryptic passages from the Old Testament and claiming that they clearly are speaking about Jesus. I do believe, however, that the above progression of faith from Noah to

Abraham to Moses reveals the logical next step in God's plan. Just as Moses was willing to sacrifice himself in an attempt to redeem the sinful Israelites, Jesus demonstrated the next logical step in God's plan by sacrificing himself in order to redeem the Gentiles who stood outside of the covenant of Israel, but who were prepared to repent and believe in the one God.

In the story of Jonah, God Himself despaired over Jonah when he seemed more upset over the death of the large plant which had shaded him outside of Nineveh than for the lives of the Gentiles of Nineveh. God chided Jonah, saying in Jonah 4:11 [Sinai Tanakh]: "And should not I spare Nineveh, that great city, wherein are more than six score thousand persons that cannot discern between their right hand and their left hand...?" The reference to the Gentiles of Nineveh not knowing their right hand from their left probably refers to the Ninevites' ignorance of the religious significance of the right hand. The Jewish Sages believed that the Torah was given by God with His right hand, based on Deuteronomy 33:2 [Sinai Tanakh], "The Lord came from Sinai ...from his right hand went a fiery law for them." Also, Jews traditionally entered the Temple from the right side and the mezuzah is placed on the right doorpost[187]. Not knowing the right hand from the left signifies the lack of knowledge of God.

The book of Jonah makes clear God's desire that Israel bring the Gentiles to God, a desire which is acknowledged in some of the most important Jewish prayers. Perhaps the best-known prayer of Judaism, the *Kaddish*, is said by mourners for the dead. And yet the Kaddish (literally "holy" in Aramaic), although intended to elevate the soul of the deceased[188], deals not with death, but rather is a declaration of faith and recognition of Israel's national purpose - that God's "great name be exalted and sanctified in the world He created."[189]. As Rabbi Donin has noted:

> "Its [the Kaddish's] opening words, yitgadal v'yitkadash...were inspired by Ezekiel 38:23, where the prophet envisions a time when God will become great and hallowed in the eyes of all nations; they shall learn 'that I am the Lord'."[190].

In another Jewish prayer, the *Aleinu*, which is the closing prayer of each daily service throughout the year, the worshippers acknowledge Israel's distinctive role among the nations of the world, but then, as Rabbi Donin describes:

> "The second paragraph anticipates sharing this distinction with all the nations of the earth. We look forward to the day when all men will worship the One Universal God, not necessarily by converting to Judaism but by acknowledging His sovereignty. Only then (with the acceptance of the ethical duties that flow from that acknowledgment) will mankind be perfected."[191].

It has also been noted that:

"The concept and goal of worldwide recognition of Hashem [God] is one of the Torah's basic tenets. It is mentioned in our prayers at least seven times a day."[192].

The wish of the Kaddish and the Aleinu that all nations come to worship God matches the beginning of the Lord's Prayer, taught by Jesus to his disciples:

"Our Father, who art in heaven,
hallowed be thy name.
Thy kingdom come,
Thy will be done,
on earth as it is in heaven...."
(Matthew 6:9-13)

In the Kaddish, the Aleinu and the Lord's Prayer, belief in God appears to be the critical force which brings into actuality the Kingdom of God on earth. As one midrash expresses this concept:

"Until Abraham, our father, came to the world, the Holy One, blessed be He, was (as it were) only king of heaven, for it is written, 'The Lord, the God of heaven, who took me...' (Gen. 24.7). But when Abraham, our father, came into the world, he made him king over heaven and earth, for it is written 'I will make you swear by the Lord, the God of heaven and of the earth' (Gen. 24.2)"[193].

The Didache (The Teachings of the Twelve Apostles)

As further evidence that the early disciples of Jesus did not understand Jesus to be advocating any abolishment of Mosaic law, but rather the expansion of Mosaic law to cover the Gentiles to the extent possible, readers need only look at the Didache (pronounced did-uh-kay), otherwise known as The Teaching of the Twelve Apostles[194]. The Didache is a composite document, the critical sections of which may have been written between around 60 C.E. and the early part of the second century C.E. The first part of the Didache may have been based in part on an earlier Jewish model[195]. The Didache is of great importance because it is the oldest surviving piece of non-canonical literature and because it was designed to instruct Gentile converts in the core elements of the Christian faith. The Didache is divided into three sections (a first (and possibly oldest) section containing catechetical lessons, a second section containing descriptions of Christian liturgy, such as baptism, fasting and communion, and a third section on church organization). It is important to note the following portions of the Didache which, although clearly evidencing that a split had arisen between the first and second century Christian and Jewish communities, still confirms the close connection between early Christianity and Temple Judaism:

(A) echoing Deuteronomy 11:26-28, where Moses sets a blessing and a curse before the Israelites, a blessing if they obey God's commandments and a curse it they do not, the Didache states that there are Two Ways, one of life (if one loves God the creator and follows the golden rule and the ten commandments, which are discussed in some detail) and one of death, where one does not: Didache, I-V

(B) citing to Deuteronomy 4:2, the Didache states that "Thou shalt not forsake the commandments of the Lord, but thou shalt keep what thou didst receive, '*adding nothing to it and taking nothing away*'", confirming the early Christians' belief that Jesus had not advocated the abandonment of Mosaic law or taught the invalidity of Mosaic law: Didache IV(13)

(C) the Didache contains a weak reference to the rules against eating non-kosher food, but stresses the Jewish prohibition against eating foods sanctified to idols, stating that "concerning food, bear what thou canst, but keep strictly from that which is offered to idols, for it is the worship of dead gods": Didache, VI(3)

(D) the Didache states that baptism was to be done in running water (i.e. "living water" acceptable for Jewish ritual immersion)[196], if possible: Didache VIII (1)

(E) the Didache evokes the Jewish practice of fasting, stating, however, that while Jews fasted on Mondays and Thursdays, Christians should fast on Wednesdays and Fridays

(F) with wording evoking the Jewish blessing said over wine[197], the grace over the Eucharist contained in the Didache reaffirms the Jewish roots of Christianity, stating "We give thanks to thee, our Father, for the Holy Vine of David they child, which thou didst make known to us through Jesus thy child; to thee be glory for ever." : Didache IX(1 -2)

(G) the grace said over the bread in the Didache evokes the Jewish prayers for God to collect up the faithful, scattered over the earth[198], reading "We give thee thanks, our Father, for the life and knowledge which thou didst make known to us through Jesus thy child, to thee be glory for ever. As this broken bread was scattered upon the mountains, but was brought together and become one, so let thy Church be gathered together from the ends of the earth into thy kingdom, for thine is the glory and the power through Jesus Christ for ever.": Didache IX(3-4)

(H) Just as devout Jews said a blessing after a meal (*Birkat haMazon*)[199], the Didache provides for a grace after the Eucharist, where the worshippers give thanks "for the immortality which thou didst make known to us through Jesus thy child" and for giving "eternal light through thy Child"; the worshippers also say "Hosannah to the God of David", all confirming that the God of Christians is the same God as the God of the Jews, that Jesus was seen as the son of God, but not a second Godhead and that Jesus was the "eternal light" which taught the worshippers about immortality: Didache XI (1-6)

(I) echoing continued reverence for *Shavuot*, the Jewish festival of first fruits[200] and one of the three pilgrimage festivals to the Second Temple, the Didache states "Therefore thou shalt take the firstfruit of the produce of the winepress and of the threshing-floor and of oxen and sheep, and shalt give them as the firstfruits to the prophets, for they are your high priests. But if you have not a prophet, give to the poor...give according to the commandment": Didache XII (3-7); and

(J) the Didache states that one should confess transgressions and reconcile with fellow worshippers with whom one has quarreled before partaking in the Eucharist, so "that your sacrifice not be defiled", indicating that the Eucharist was viewed by early worshippers as akin to a sin-offering sacrifice at the Second Temple, with Jesus' sacrifice taking the place of the sacrificial offering of the Temple worshipper.

God as an Example for the Israelites/
Jesus as a Living Example for Gentiles

God Himself acts as an example for the Israelites in the Torah. As the Jewish Sage Rabbi Hama expounded on Deuteronomy 13:5 ("Follow the Lord, your God"):

"Is it possible for a man to follow the Shekhinah [the Divine Presence]? Is it not written, 'The Lord your God is a devouring fire' (Deut. 4.24)? But follow the attributes (qualities) of the Holy one blessed be he. Since he clothes the naked, as it is written, 'And the Lord God made for Adam and his wife garments of skin and clothed them' (Gen. 3.21), you too must clothe the naked. Since the Holy one blessed be he visited the sick, as it is written, 'And the Lord appeared to him (Abraham after his circumcision) at the Oaks of Mamre' (Gen. 18.1), you too must visit the sick. Since the Holy one blessed be he comforted the mourners, as it is written, 'After the death of Abraham God blessed his son Isaac' (Gen. 25.11), you too must comfort the mourners. Since the Holy one blessed be he buried the dead, as it is written, 'And he buried him (Moses) in the valley' (Deut. 34.6), you too must bury the dead (bSotah 14a)"[201].

Since the nation of Israel, like Jonah, so far has not been destined to be a major proselytizing force in the world, is it not possible that the object sought by the Kaddish and the

Aleinu- that the entire world sanctify God's great name - required that God's light, set aside from the first day of creation, be born a man and live for a time on earth, as a messenger of God's love to all Gentiles who would repent and place their trust in God. Is it not possible that the light of the first day of creation was sent by God **to be as a living example to Gentiles of what it means to be created in the image of God and lead a life that exalts and sanctifies God's great name? Is this what Jesus meant when he said: "...for behold the Kingdom of God [*i.e., Jesus as the light from the world to come*] is in the midst of you" (Luke 17:20)?**.

That Jesus taught salvation through his teaching and by example can be seen from the "Beatitudes" ("... Blessed are the merciful, for they shall obtain mercy. Blessed are the pure in heart, for they shall see God....") and from his depiction of judgment day when those who fed and clothed the poor, cared for the sick and visited those in prison are treated as if they had done the same for Jesus himself, and thereby merit salvation in the world to come (Matthew 25:34-46).

**The Temple High Priest as
a Benchmark for the Disciples**

Jesus also may have used the high level of spiritual purity binding only on the High Priest of the Temple as an example of the high level of dedication which Jesus expected of his followers. Thus, when Jesus tells his disciples that divorce is prohibited (Matthew 5:31-32), this would mirror the disqualification from priesthood in the Temple of those who were born from a divorced mother. Also, Jesus tells a disciple, who has asked to leave Jesus to bury his father, "Leave the dead to bury their own dead; but as for you, go and proclaim the Kingdom of God." (Luke 9:59-60; Matthew 8:21-22). This would mirror the prohibition on the High Priest of leaving his service to God to bury his parents[202]. Unless these sayings of Jesus are seen as an indirect reference to the standards of dedication to God by which the High Priest was bound, the sayings appear to directly violate the Ten Commandments (e.g., the Fifth Commandment to honor one's father and mother) and the Torah (e.g., the requirement to bury the dead; the provision for granting a divorce through a "*Get*" (Deut. 24:1-4)) and would have been highly offensive to his followers. Also, just as the Priests were not allowed to own land and lived off the tithing of the Israelites, eating the food offered up for sacrifice, so Jesus' disciples were taught to pursue a life free of material possessions.

The High Priest of the Temple wore a golden headband tied around his head covering which said "HOLINESS UNTO THE LORD". Jesus expected his disciples to view themselves as similarly dedicated to God's exclusive service. However, unlike the High Priest, who wore bells on the hem of his robe in order to warn others of his approach so that ritually impure individuals would not accidentally touch him and render him incapable of performing the Temple service, Jesus' disciples were being readied to go out into the world as missionaries (Luke 9:1-6). Indeed, the land outside of *Eretz Yisrael*, the land of the Israelites, was ritually impure and setting foot on the soil or breathing the air outside of *Eretz Yisrael* automatically made one ritually impure[203]. Therefore, Jesus de-emphasized the need to strictly follow the Mosaic rules with respect to ritual impurity, eating impure foods and the prohibition against work on the Sabbath - rules which could easily be followed within a tight-knit Jewish community, but could be very difficult to follow far from *Eretz Yisrael* in the midst of Gentile communities. As Jesus points out, just as the Priests are permitted to work in the Temple on the Sabbath in God's service, so he expects his disciples to work out in the world saving sinners and bringing them to God (Mark 12:5). Jesus' apostles were sent out into the pagan world to accomplish the vision of Zechariah 14:20-21, where the prophet describes the time when all the nations will come to the Temple to worship the Feast of Sukkot and "In that day shall there be upon the bells of the horses [*an inscription identical to the High Priest's plate, reading*], HOLINESS UNTO THE LORD...and every pot in Jerusalem and in Judah shall be holiness unto the Lord of hosts [*i.e., every pot will be as holy as the offering bowls in front of the Temple altar*]...and in that day there shall be no more a merchant in the house of the Lord of hosts [i.e., *no moneychangers on the temple mount*]" [Zechariah 14:20-21: Sinai Tanakh][explanatory note added in italics].

Jesus also emphasizes, by example, the spreading of God's word through easily understood parables rather than through detailed analyses of the Torah, because the Gentiles are to be the intended audience of the disciples, not the existing Jewish communities which were learned in Torah. It is also noteworthy that although Jesus explained the true meaning of his parables to his faithful disciples, he did not explain them to the crowds of people who listened to him as he preached in the countryside (Matthew 13:10-15). This parallels God's gift of manna in the desert, where the manna fell directly in front of the tents of the righteous, while the average Israelite had to go about to gather the manna and the wicked Israelites had to search hard for the manna[204].

In one sense, the mission of Jesus also can be better understood in first century Jewish terms when compared to the significance of the High Priest for the devout Jew. Traditionally, if a man killed another man unintentionally, the accused was allowed to escape to a so-called "city of refuge", where the victim's family was prohibited from taking vengeance on him. The thirteen cities of refuge were the original inheritance of the tribe of Levi (the tribe of Priests), bequeathed to them by Jacob on his deathbed, and the cities were spread throughout Israel[205]. Only upon the death of the High Priest was the accused allowed to return from the City of Refuge, free of further punishment[206]. In a sense, Jesus' sacrifice of himself allowed sinners to return to God and the community of the righteous, just as the death of the High Priest marked the time of expiation of the guilt of the man who committed manslaughter.

Finally, Jesus emphasizes the need to quickly repent and return to God. Modern-day critics point to this as evidence that since the end of the world was not actually near, Jesus could not have been sent by God but must have been just a charismatic healer-teacher-prophet with eschatological leanings[207]. I do not agree with this position. Jesus was frank in stating that the day and hour of the arrival of the world to come was unknown to Jesus and was known only to God (see, e.g., Matthew 24:36). Jesus may have had a very good reason to emphasize that time was short to his followers, even though he admittedly did not know when the world to come would occur. As has been recounted in a popular book on the Ten Commandments[208]:

> *"There is an old story that one day Satan gathered his assistants to discuss the most effective method of destroying the meaning of people's lives. One suggested, 'Tell them there is no God.' Another said, 'Tell them there are no consequences to their actions.' A third proposed, 'Tell them they have strayed so far from the right path they will never be able to change.' 'No,' Satan replied, 'such things will not matter to them. I think we should simply tell them, 'There is plenty of time'.'"*

Jesus' message was clear and wholly appropriate to prepare his apostles to go out into the world and save sinners' souls: do not believe Satan - there is not "plenty of time".

Understanding the Last Supper (Eucharist) and Baptism through Reference to Temple Ritual

The two key sacraments which Jesus instituted for his apostles (and which the apostles later instituted for the Christian church) are the Eucharist and baptism. Both can perhaps be better understood and appreciated if their roots in Judaism are recognized. As Rev. William Harter has noted:

> *"Today Christian scholars understand that Jewish liturgy and festivals had a profound impact on the writing of the Gospels and on the modes of worship in the early church. They see that the early church leaders followed some of the same methods of explaining the Hebrew Bible as the rabbis. The scholars are now able to see how the Jewish background and exposure to Jewish life of the authors of the New Testament molded their thinking."*[209].

It has also been noted that:

> *"... [A]n inability to understand our Jewish roots has the effect of diminishing our grasp and appreciation of the Church's liturgical practice, which is largely an inheritance from Judaism (CCC, 1096)"*[210].

The Eucharist and the Temple Offering

The Last Supper of Jesus with his disciples (possibly a Seder in celebration of the Passover) can also be understood better if the disciples of Jesus are seen in the mold of Priests of the Temple. The Priests in the Temple each week ate the twelve loaves ("*Challah*") of Shewbread (the "*Lechem Hapanim*" or literally the "Face [*panim*] of God", meaning the "presence" of God) consecrated in the Sanctuary of the Temple to God (Leviticus 24:5-9). Similarly, Jesus asked his twelve disciples to eat the bread of the Last Supper, which he had blessed, saying "Take, eat; this is my body" (Matthew 26:26; Mark 14:22; Luke 22:19). With respect to the wine, Jesus says "Drink it, all of you, for this is my blood of the covenant, which is **poured out** for many for the forgiveness of sins [emphasis added]" (Matthew 26:27-28; Mark 14:22). The phrasing adopted by Jesus might have evoked to the disciples the image of the Priest in the Temple pouring out the blood of the sacrifice on the altar[211]. Jews believed that the spirit of life was in the blood and that it was strictly forbidden by the Torah to eat a creature while still alive (with its blood in it) or even to eat blood after being taken from the creature, the penalty for which was automatic "*karais*" (excision) from God and the Jewish people.[212] Accordingly, I assume that the disciples understood the wine to be symbolic of sacrificial blood poured out on the Temple altar, since drinking actual blood would have been in direct contravention of the Torah and would have horrified Jesus' Jewish disciples, since drinking it would have meant immediate excision from God and the community.

That the Eucharist is a symbolic remembrance of Jesus' sacrifice of himself rather than intended to be the actual consumption of bread and wine transformed supernaturally into human flesh and blood is also evident from the fact that (a) the gospel of Luke does not describe any offering of wine, but only an offering of bread as representing the body of Jesus, which should be eaten, Jesus says, "in remembrance of me" (Luke 22:19 footnote J) and (b) the gospel of John does not describe the offering of bread and wine at all (see John 19:14). Further, as noted above in the Didache, the bread signified scattered people restored to unity at the end of time.[213] If the bread and wine had been seen by the early disciples as anything other than a symbolic ritual, all four gospels would likely have highlighted the event and explained it in more detail.

I cannot speak to the validity or non-validity of the Catholic doctrine of "transubstantiation" (where the Eucharistic wafer and wine at Mass is believed to be transformed into the body and blood of Christ). I can only note that this concept would likely have been very difficult for the original Jewish disciples to have accepted and still have returned to worship at the Temple, as they reportedly did upon the resurrection of Jesus. In order to harmonize transubstantiation with the precepts of Judaism, the bread and wine would have to be transformed into the divine aspect of Jesus as the light from the world to come (akin to the shewbread being the "*lechem hapanim*", representing the "face" or "presence" of God for the

Temple priests), not Jesus' actual flesh and blood.

It should be noted, however, that the communion represented more than just a symbolic remembrance of Jesus to the apostles. The apostles and the church they created believed that the Eucharist represented the one perfect sacrifice made by Jesus for the atonement and forgiveness of his followers' sins. For the devout Jewish apostles, who were familiar with bringing lambs, goats and bullocks to the Temple to be sacrificed as offerings in their places in atonement for their sins, the act of Jesus in voluntarily giving himself up to be crucified may have evoked the image of the Temple sin offerings. Since they believed Jesus to be of divine origin, they may have believed that Jesus' sacrifice could atone for all who believed in him, whether currently living or yet to be born. ***In the Temple, the sin-offering was not valid unless the offeror was present (or had a representative present)***[214]. ***The Eucharist was the ritualistic Temple equivalent of being present at the sacrifice of Jesus, so as to be part of (and thus benefit from) the offering.***

Although the Christian Church adopted some of the Passover (Pesach) terminology for the Christian "Principal Feast" of Easter, calling Jesus the "Pascal Lamb", the Didache shows that the sacrifices most likely evoked for the apostles were the daily Temple sin-offerings of lambs. In the days of the Second Temple, the sacrifice of the Pesach lamb was a sacrifice of "lesser holiness", while the daily sacrifice of lambs as sin offerings and the sacrifice of the bulls at Sukkot were sacrifices of "higher holiness"[215]. The types of animals permitted to be sacrificed (lambs, doves, cattle) were all domesticated, peaceful creatures, the hunted rather than the hunters (eagles, lions, etc.)[216]. Similarly, Jesus, the Lamb of God, taught pacifism and told his followers to "turn the other cheek". The Priests at the Temple ate the birds, lambs, rams, oxen, bread and wine given as sin (*Chatas*), guilt (*Asham*), peace (*Shlamim*) and meal (*Mincha*) offerings, with only the *Olah* (voluntary burnt offering not given to atone for any sins) not being eaten by the Priests[217]. Similarly, Jesus' disciples as his priests were to eat the bread and wine as ritualistic participants of Jesus' sacrifice of himself to atone for their sins.

Finally, in order to understand the powerful impact which the sacrifice and resurrection of Jesus had on his disciples, many of whom were devout Jews who worshipped at the Second Temple, one need only bring to mind the significance of the ritual sacrifices of the Second Temple. As Rabbi Ira Stone has noted[218]:

> *"Sacrifice was the highest form of worship in the Bible and was treated as such by subsequent Jewish commentators...we [must] suspend contemporary distaste for actual animal sacrifice and discover the theology which sustained this institution and made remembering it so important in Jewish liturgy long after the Temple in Jerusalem had ceased to exist. In sacrifice we could, for a fleeting moment, imagine our own death and,*

yet, go on living. No other form of worship can bring a person so near to the prospect of death. Therefore, no other form of worship can so effectively liberate a person from the fear of living in the shadow of death. Worshippers came to the Temple to dispel their terror of death's solitude by conjuring a moment in which they shared the experience of death with God. But strictly speaking, death shared with God is no longer death, for there is no death in God. The experience of death which is no longer death sustains for the worshipper the promise of immortal life."

Baptism and the Jewish Ritual Immersion

The second sacrament, baptism, can also be better understood against the backdrop of Judaism. It was traditional for devout Jews to immerse themselves in rivers, pools (*Mikveh*) of rain water or other "living waters" in order to purify themselves. John the Baptist was a devout Jew, the son of a Temple priest (Luke 1:5), who encouraged this practice of ritual immersion for spiritual purification[219]. The concept of immersion in "living waters" in order to remove ritual impurities derives from Leviticus 11:36 [Koren Tanakh]:"...Nevertheless, a fountain or pit, wherein there is a collection [mikveh] of water shall be clean." The Mikveh also symbolized "hope" to the early Jewish community. As is stated in the Talmud[220]:

> *"The word 'mikveh' is a homonym meaning both 'fountain', thus ritual bath, and 'hope'."*

Christians need to fully appreciate the Jewish context of "living waters" in order to understand what Jesus was offering -that to believe in him was akin to immersion in "living waters" ("*mayim chayim*" in Hebrew) - because it would remove one's sins and offer hope in place of despair, life in place of death. This can be seen in the Didache, the training manual of the early Christian Church discussed above, which advises that baptism should be done in "running water"[221].

Jesus himself was baptized by John at the start of his active ministry (Matthew 3:13; Mark 1:9; Luke 3:21). John the Baptist at first balks at baptizing Jesus, but Jesus insists that he be immersed in the river Jordan in order "for us to fulfil all righteousness" (Matthew 3:13-14). Unlike the baptism given by John to devout Jews for the temporary cleansing of sin, Jesus' baptism by John, the son of the Temple Priest, evokes the immersion in "living waters" of all of the vessels to be used in the Temple at the time of their initial dedication, such as the sacrificial cups and the curtain which hid the Holy of Holies[222]. Jesus' baptism represented his dedication to God's service as a vessel of God's will. While Jews enter into their covenant with God through circumcision ("*bris*"), Christians adapted the ritual immersion to mark their covenant with God through Jesus, their "death" to a life of sin and rebirth to a new life, dedicated to the service of God. Just as the circumcision is a one-time ritual, the Jewish ritual immersion was made a one-time baptism for the Christian covenantal ritual.

In Judaism, a proselyte or convert undergoes a ritual immersion in a mikveh[223] and is deemed to have died and been reborn upon conversion, with the result that the convert has the legal status of a newborn child[224]. The early Christians, who were devout Jews, may have adapted this belief to fit the ritual immersion, so that through baptism, converts to Christianity entered into their covenant with the God of Israel and were purified and reborn as Christians. The "born-again Christian" therefore is not so far removed in theological terms from the Jewish proselyte, who was a heathen but is reborn a Jew and who has the legal status of a new-born child.

The Divine Missionary

God performed many miracles in the presence of the Israelites, many of which were individually and immediately felt by each Israelite. As is noted in one midrash:

> *"At the place named Mai Meriva, Moshe and Aharon assembled the entire nation in front of a rock from which the almighty would bring forth water. At that time, a miracle occurred. Every single Jew actually found himself standing in front of the rock (Bamidbar 20:20)"*[225].

In the above "Drash", God miraculously places the water-giving rock directly in front of each Israelite. Does the story of Jesus indicate that God decided, if Gentiles would not come to Him, ***that He would send the light from the world to come to be a missionary to them***?

Devout Jews believe that Shabbat, the Sabbath, is but a taste of the world to come for Jews who are faithful to the Torah[226]. Death therefore holds no fears for devout Jews, since they believe in resurrection of the faithful in the world to come. As it is written in Ezekiel 37:12: "Behold, O my people, I will open your graves, and cause you to come up out of your graves, and bring you into the land of Israel." [Sinai Tanakh]

Philip Yancy gives a wonderful explanation of how the book of Job, one of the oldest books in the Tanakh, evidences God's promise of the world to come:

> *"Having no clearly formed belief in an afterlife, Job's friends wrongly assumed that God's fairness - his approval or disapproval of people - had to be shown in this life only. Other parts of the Bible teach that God will mete out justice after death. The pleasure that Job enjoyed in his old age is a mere foretaste of what is to come. The author of Job*

42 includes one poignant detail. All of Job's material possessions are doubled in his old age. Once owner of 7,000 sheep, 3,000 camels, 500 yoke of oxen, and 500 donkeys, he now possesses 14,000 sheep, 6,000 camels, 1,000 yoke of oxen, and 1,000 donkeys. Significantly, though, his family does not double. The father of seven sons and three daughters becomes father of seven new sons and three new daughters - not fourteen sons and six daughters. Even in the middle of the Old Testament, which has a shadowy concept of the afterlife at best, the book of Job clearly intimates that Job will one day get his original family back. The ten children he tragically lost will be restored to him, to live in glorious eternity in a redeemed and recreated world."[227]

Indeed, the book of Job in stirring and vivid poetic language contrasts Job's evocation of nihilism and darkness in his death-wish poem of Chapter 3 with God's affirmation of life and rebirth in Chapters 38 and 39. As Robert Alter has noted[228]:

"In both structure and thematic assertion, Chapters 31-41 are a great diastolic movement, responding to the systolic movement of Chapter 3. The poetics of suffering in Chapter 3 seeks to contract the whole world to a point of extinction, and it generates a chain of images of enclosure and restriction. The poetics of providential vision in the speech from the storm [God] conjures up horizon after expanding horizon, each populated with a new form of life...In Chapter 3, only in the grave did prisoners 'no longer hear the taskmaster's voice' (3:18), and only there was 'the slave free of his master' (3:19). But this, God's rejoinder implies, is a civilization-bound, hobbled perception of reality, for nature abounds in images of freedom: 'Who set the wild ass free,/who undid the bonds of the onager,//Whose home I made in the steppes,/his dwelling-place the salt land?//He scoffs at the bustle of the city,/the shouts of the taskmaster he does not hear' (39:5-7)...God's poetry enables Job to glimpse beyond his human plight an immense world of power and beauty and awesome warring forces. This world is permeated with God's ordering concern, but as the vividness of the verse makes clear, it presents to the human eye a welter of contradictions, dizzying variety, energies and entities that man cannot take in...[C]reation can perhaps be sensed but not encompassed by the mind - like that final image of the crocodile [Leviathan] already whipping away from our field of vision, leaving behind only a shining wake for us to see."

Jesus also confirmed the truth that the God of Israel is a God of life and not of death and that the grave is not the path to "freedom" as evoked by the suffering Job. Instead, Jesus taught the triumph over death through faith in the one God, saying:

"But that the dead are raised even Moses showed, in the passage about the burning bush,

where he calls the Lord the God of Abraham and the God of Isaac and the God of Jacob. Now He is not God of the dead, but of the living; for all live to him." (Luke 20:34-38).

Is it not possible that God decided to make the light of the first day of creation, **the light reserved for the world to come**, take human form and be born, suffer and die, but then rise up from the dead after three days (as Jonah was delivered to Nineveh after three days in the belly of the fish), so as to be a light for revelation to the Gentiles (those who did not "know their right hand from their left")? Is it not also possible that the revelation of Jesus to the Gentiles was of something devout Jews already knew and believed - **that repentance ("Teshuvah") and faithful trust in God leads to salvation, that men should imitate the attributes of God in their relations with each other (clothe the poor, comfort the suffering and care for the sick, etc.) and that death has no lasting dominion over those who believe in God, since they have helped create the Kingdom of God by their own faith?**

"Do This in Remembrance of Me"

Thirteen figures are stretched across a table. Christ, with bread and wine in hand. Collagraph with acrylic paint in edition of 100 16.5" x 24.5" image - Sandra Bowden

DOMINION

"It is Finished"

The crucifixion is central to Christianity. The inscription above Christ's head reads, Jesus of Nazareth, King of the Jews, written in Hebrew, Greek and Latin. Layers of fabric and other materials provide the surface texture. The crown of thorns has been constructed using old floor nails. The abstracted forms suggest the brokenness Christ endured, distorted by our sin in order to restore our relationship to God. Contained within the torso is a large arrow shape, thrusting itself into a flat broad area of red. The plate is constructed by using textured fabrics and materials adhered to a Masonite surface, then painted, and finally transferred to the paper as it is runs through an etching press. Collagraph with acrylic painting 1980 21" x 16" - Sandra Bowden

DOMINION

"There is no man that hath power over the spirit to retain the spirit;
neither hath he power in the day of death."

-Ecclesiastes 8:8 [Sinai Tanakh]

One of Rashi's most fascinating commentaries involves Exodus 2:23, where the Torah states that the King of Egypt died and the Israelites groaned and cried out to God. Rashi's commentary interprets the text as actually meaning that the King had developed leprosy and slaughtered Israelites in order to bathe in their blood to try and cure his leprosy. Avigdor Bonchek[229] explains Rashi's comment by noting that if the text were taken literally, the Israelites would have rejoiced over the King's death, not groaned and cried out to God. Bonchek cites to the Talmudic statement[230], that one with leprosy is considered as dead, as support for Rashi's analysis. Bonchek then cites the Gaon of Vilna[231] for the further explanation that Ecclesiastes 8:8 states that there is no dominion on the day of death, meaning that when a King dies, he no longer has any special powers since death is the great equalizer. Thus, when King David dies (1 Kings 2), the Bible refers to him solely as "David", without his title. Bonchek notes that this rule is consistently followed throughout the Torah. If the King of Egypt had literally died, he would have been referred to by his name only and not as a king.

Jesus' Dominion over Death

Keeping this concept in mind, think of how Jesus is described in the gospels of Matthew, Mark and Luke, the oldest of the gospels. As is exhaustively analyzed by Geza Vermes[232], Jesus did not assume the attitude of a king or assume that title. Indeed, Vermes analyzes the probable original meanings of titles applied to Jesus in the gospels, such as "prophet", "lord", "son of man" and "son of God", and makes a persuasive argument that even when Jesus was given these titles, they probably did not signify the power and dominion resonating from the current usage of the titles, but rather had more neutral meanings. This analysis is consistent with John 6:15:

"Perceiving then that they were about to come and take him by force and make him king, Jesus withdrew again to the hills by himself."

This is also consistent with the total lack of concern shown by Jesus for the perceived spiritual impurity (under Jewish law) that he would suffer by touching lepers in order to heal them (Matthew 8:3-4), by allowing sinners to anoint him (Luke 7:39), and by touching the dead (Luke 8:54). As Jesus says to his apostles: "For the Son of man also came not to be served but to serve, and to give his life as a ransom for many." (Mark 10:45). It is also consistent with Jesus' pacifism, urging his followers to turn the other cheek when confronted with force (Matthew 5:38) and saying that "Blessed are the peacemakers" (Matthew 5:9).

Psalm 22: All the Ends of the World
Shall Turn to the Lord

When Jesus is dying on the cross, he cries out in Aramaic: *"Eli, Eli, lama sabachthani ("My God, my God, why hast thou forsaken me?)"* (Matthew 27:46; Mark 15:34) - the opening line of Psalm 22 [Koren Tanakh]. Psalm 22 is noted in commentaries, because it refers to the speaker (a) as being surrounded by people mocking him, saying "He trusts in the Lord that he will deliver him? Let him deliver him seeing he delights in him." (b) as being laid "down in the dust of death", (c) as having his hands and feet "seized" as if he "were a lion", and (d) seeing his tormentors casting lots for his garments [Koren Tanakh]. Of more significance, however, are the closing lines of Psalm 22 where the speaker of the Psalm asks for God to deliver him, saying that then [Psalm 22:28-29]:

"All the ends of the world shall remember and turn to the Lord: and all the families of the nations shall worship before thee. For the kingdom is the Lord's: and he is ruler over the nations." (Koren Tanakh)

Remembering that Jesus had told all of his disciples that he would die, but would rise again from the dead (Mark 8:31, 9:31, 10:34, 16:6-7, Matthew 26:64, Luke 24:6-7), the fact that Matthew and Mark both recount the last words of Jesus as coming from Psalm 22 may relate not only to how Psalm 22 mirrors the circumstances of Jesus' death (as noted in (a)-(d) above), but also to the ***intended result*** of Jesus' deliverance from death: all the ends of the earth and all of the nations would recognize that Jesus had established dominion over death and therefore rightfully was to now be called King and Lord, titles he rejected before his death. This explains the paradox of Jesus consistently refusing to acknowledge that he was the Jewish Messiah who would through military success bring about an independent Israel (Mark 8:31-33; Matthew 26:64), while at the same time deliberately having planned an entry into Jerusalem as the humble, but triumphant king prophesied in Zechariah 9:9 (see Mark 11:1-7; Matthew 21:1-7; Luke 19:29- 35).

Some of the disciples of Jesus may have been zealots, formerly dedicated to the violent overthrow of the Roman occupation forces. For example, the apostle Simon is identified as Simon the Zealot (see Luke 6:15). One commentator has also surmised that Judas Iscariot may have been originally named Judas Sicarius, so-named because the zealots were call "Sicarii", Latin for "assassin", a term sometimes applied to Zealots who killed Jewish collaborators[233].

Judas may have thought that Jesus' triumphal entry into Jerusalem was the start of his organization of a military force, only to be bitterly disappointed when it became obvious that Jesus was not going to lead any uprising against the Roman forces. This may explain Judas' betrayal of Jesus as being politically motivated rather than being inspired merely by the greedy wish for a payment of 30 pieces of silver[234]. For example, if Judas had handed Jesus over to the authorities out of disgust with Jesus' failure to act as a military leader against the Roman occupation, his pacifism and his washing of the disciples' feet (a task normally undertaken only by a slave[235]), then Judas' request for payment, which results in his receiving 30 pieces of silver (see Matthew 26:14-16), might be understandable. According to Rabbinic interpretation of Leviticus 27:1-8, damages required to be paid for an ox goring a man was 50 shekels, while a woman or a slave would be worth only 30 shekels in damages[236]. By taking only 30 shekels, Judas the Zealot was implicitly condemning Jesus as having acted like a woman or a slave, rather than as a real man.

It was only after Jesus rose from the dead that his followers recognized that Jesus deliberately spurned kingship and dominion (and the role of the traditional military-political Jewish Messiah) during his life, but earned the title of "King of kings and Lord of lords" by establishing his dominion over death in the face of Ecclesiastes 8:8. Thus, when Jesus meets his disciple Thomas after Jesus is risen from the dead and Jesus tells Thomas that he is risen in the flesh and offers to let Thomas touch his wounds, Thomas exclaims to Jesus for the first time: "My Lord and my God!" (John 20:28).

Ecclesiastes 8:8 therefore can be seen to be the pivotal passage which divides the two religions of Judaism and Christianity. For although Judaism and Christianity comprise one faith, both believing in the God of Israel, the devout Jew reads Ecclesiastes 8:8 and says: yes, it is true! For the devout Jew, great prophets may be taken by God to the world to come without dying (e.g., as occurred with Enoch and Elijah (Genesis 5:24; 2 Kings 2:11-18)), but bodily resurrection from the dead could only occur with the coming of the Day of Judgment and the world to come[237].

The devout Christian, however, reads Ecclesiastes 8:8 and says: yes, *it is true for man,* but Jesus is the light of God given to be born, suffer and die as a man for the salvation of the Gentiles - just as the sacrificial goat of Azazel atoned for Israel's sins on the Day of Atonement - and Jesus is risen!

The Death and Resurrection as Proof of the Truth of the World to Come

While Jesus in his lifetime taught in parables and performed healing in order to show the Gentiles the **nature of the world to come** (faith and repentance leads to healing and purification), Jesus by his death and resurrection showed the Gentiles the **truth of the world to come**. That Christians view the resurrection as the keystone of their religion is evident from the fact that Easter Day, the day of the resurrection of Jesus, is a moveable "Principal Feast" of the Church which occurs on the first Sunday after the full moon that falls on or after March 21st and the sequence of all other Sundays in the Church year depend on the date of Easter for that year[238].

And yet this division over the resurrection of Jesus between Judaism and Christianity may also be God's will and something to be preserved at all cost. As one Jewish commentator wrote:

> *"The Netziv (She'eiris Yisrael) notes that Scripture uses fire as a metaphor for Israel (Obadiah 1:18) and water to describe the gentile nations (Song of Songs 8:7). When water is placed upon fire with a barrier (i.e. a pot) separating them, the fire will warm the water, which in turn can cook food or serve some other beneficial purpose. However, when the two come in direct contact with one another, co-existence is impossible; the water douses the fire. So, too, says the Netziv, is it with Israel and the nations. The Jewish people have much to offer the world as a light unto the nations, but to fulfill this role, they must remain distinct. It is absolutely essential that the Jewish people maintain their pure faith, fidelity to Torah and distinct way of life. If, however, they lose their distinctiveness, then their fire becomes nothing more than useless, suffocating smoke."*[239].

Indeed, one Jewish Midrash explains that heaven itself was formed from fire and water:

> *"Upon completing the firmament [on the second day of creation], Hashem named it shamayim/heaven. The name shamayim reveals the secret of the substances from which it was fashioned -fire/aish and water/mayim, combining to form the composite, shamayim/heaven. Fire represents the Attribute of Justice. Water stands for the quality of Mercy. The heaven which is the residence of Hashem's glory is comprised of a combination of these two attributes."*[240].

In a sense, the redemption of the people of Israel illustrates God's infinite Justice, rewarding His chosen people for their faithful honoring of the commandments of the Torah despite being scattered amongst the nations and despite centuries of persecution. The redemption of the Gentile Christians through the perfect sacrifice made by Jesus evidences God's infinite Mercy.

Three Prophets: Isaiah, Jeremiah and Ezekiel

This triptych alludes, through the use of color, to three Old Testament
prophets and their relationship to the cities they inhabited by focusing on
their walls. Raised from the surface of the dark paper are small segments of
ancient biblical walls: Isaiah's wall of the golden city of Jerusalem; Jeremiah,
the weeping prophet's wall of Jerusalem on fire; and Ezekiel's wall of Babylon
with the intense ceramic blue which adorned its city's entrance. Collagraph in
three panels 1986 26" x 20" - Sandra Bowden

Epilogue: Holy Scripture as a "Tree of Life"

Judaism and Christianity's Combined Story of God's Will for the World

I personally accept that the Synoptic gospels (Matthew, Mark and Luke) may have evolved from earlier oral traditions and source material and that passages of the New Testament may to a certain extent represent later accretions or superimposed Church doctrine developed not by Jesus, but by his later disciples. However, in this book I have tried to take the scriptures of the New Testament at face value for the most part (especially the sections which indicate that Jesus upheld the validity of the covenant with Israel), looking to see how the story of the New Testament holds together if viewed from the perspective of the devout first century Jews who were Jesus' first apostles.

Viewed from that vantage point, I believe that Judaism and Christianity together tell a combined story of God's will for the world which is understandable and believable. I also believe that the Tanakh and the New Testament (when viewed against Jewish beliefs and practices) can continue to yield fresh insights to the determined reader. I am not a Biblical scholar and do not pretend to have any Biblical training. My goal is merely to show that even someone as unskilled as I am can reveal hidden, deeper meanings in the scriptures with determined analysis and to inspire my readers to do likewise. As the Jewish Sages taught, the Torah is a "tree of life" to those who cling to it[241]. I believe that to be equally true of the Bible for Christians.

Ultimately, belief in God and in the Jewish or Christian Holy Scriptures rests on the individual's own worldview and personal experience with God. As is evident from this book, I personally am a Christian believer in the God of Israel and recognize the validity of both the covenant of Judaism for Jews and the covenant of Jesus for Christians. Since I view God's covenant with Israel as eternally valid, I do not support aggressive missionary work from Christians to the Jewish community. The Catholic Church, for example, has given up proselytizing to Jews.[242] I believe that it is God's will that both Judaism and Christianity exist to serve His will, but as separate religions. Therefore, I personally believe that Jews who have accepted Jesus as their savior (so-called "Jews for Jesus") should be counted with the Christians and no longer should be viewed as being within the covenant of Judaism.

I personally do not believe that it is an historical accident that Judaism has survived for over 4,000 years, through the Diaspora, numerous pogroms throughout the world over the centuries and the Holocaust in the twentieth century. I also do not believe that the survival of Christianity for the past 2,000 years is an accident. I believe that God intended both religions to co-exist and that continued theological hostilities between the Christian and Jewish communities runs counter to God's will. I believe that both the Christian and Jewish communities should

82

respect each other's covenants as valid, following the advice of Rabbi Gamaliel the Elder, the teacher of the Apostle Paul (see Acts 22:3), as reported in Acts 5:35-39:

> *"Men of Israel, take care what you do with these men [the apostles]. For before these days Theudas arose, giving himself out to be somebody, and a number of men, about four hundred, joined him; but he was slain and all who followed him were dispersed and came to nothing. After him Judas the Galilean arose in the days of the census and drew away some of the people after him; he also perished, and all who followed him were scattered. So in the present case I tell you, keep away from these men and let them alone; for if this plan or this undertaking is of men, it will fail; but if it is of God, you will not be able to overthrow them. You might even be found opposing God.[emphasis added]"*

The above is also consistent with the Jewish Ethics of the Fathers (Pirkei Avot) Chapter 4:14:

> *"Rabbi Yohanan Ha-Sandlar taught: Every assembly whose purpose is to serve God will in the end be established; but every assembly whose purpose is not for God's sake, will not in the end be established."*[243]

I have attempted in this book to put flesh on the bones of ecumenical considerations through analysis and explication of both Jewish and Christian scriptures so as to demonstrate their underlying truths and make them both understandable and believable.

The Threat of Postmodernism

In today's secular world the danger exists for both Jews and Christians that they will dilute their beliefs from generation to generation, to the point where their religious beliefs look like nothing more than ethical precepts. An example of this is the work product of the Jesus Seminar, which rules out the possibility of supernatural events occurring on earth (and implicitly rules out the involvement in human affairs of the God of Israel Himself, who performed many supernatural miracles for the Israelites). As is noted in the introduction to The Jesus Seminar's The Five Gospels[244]:

> *"The Christ of creed and dogma, who had been firmly in place in the middle Ages, can no longer command the assent of those who have seen the heavens through Galileo's telescope. The old deities and demons were swept from the skies by that remarkable glass. Copernicus, Kepler, and Galileo have dismantled the mythological abodes of the gods and Satan, and bequeathed us secular heavens."*

The Jesus Seminar raises a "scientific" worldview as the standard which allegedly must be followed, and then redacts the New Testament with red, pink, gray and black markers to exclude as unhistorical anything Jesus allegedly said after his resurrection, all miraculous healing, all lengthy speeches (on the theory that only short, pithy sayings could have been remembered by Jesus' followers) and any knowledge of Torah which would have been beyond a peasant from Galilee. The Jesus Seminar thus concludes that only eighteen percent of the New Testament may possibly represent the actual teachings of Jesus. The Jesus Seminar subsequently produced The Acts of Jesus: What Did Jesus Really Do?, which examined 387 reports in the New Testament of 176 events in which Jesus was the principal actor. Again using the color ratings, the Jesus Seminar concluded that only 16% of the 176 events actually or probably occurred[245]. The logical fallacies of the Jesus Seminar (especially its reliance on a Gnostic document, The Gospel of Thomas - the Jesus Seminar's "Fifth Gospel") have already been identified by other authors to my personal satisfaction[246], so I will devote this piece to other issues.

Rather than Christianity being the greatest threat to Judaism today, I believe the greatest threat facing **both Judaism and Christianity** is the threat of being delegitimized by today's postmodernist culture and then being reduced to a matter of ethnicity (in the case of Judaism) or mere ethical precepts and social goals (in the case of Christianity). The efforts of the Jesus Seminar are ostensibly based on a "modernist" approach which applies rationality to a study of the scriptures in order to find historical "truth". In actuality, the effort is part and parcel of the "postmodernist" movement, which rejects the concept of a single objective worldview which unifies humanity. Instead, postmodernists minimize worldviews as myths or "metanarratives" constructed and revised by successive societies or groups to legitimize their belief systems and maintain social order.

This is aptly demonstrated in the debate between John Dominic Crossan, a co-Founder of the Jesus Seminar, and William Lane Craig, a leading Christian Evangelical apologist[247]. Crosson rejects the idea that God directly intervenes in the world and takes the position that Jesus did not rise from the dead. Crosson does not reject the concept of "resurrection", but he redefines it to mean that Jesus' followers experienced his presence metaphorically after Jesus' death. Crosson indicates that the supernatural is eternally present and may be glimpsed metaphorically by believers of different faiths in different ways. Thus, Crosson says that "our insistence that our faith is fact and that others' faith is a lie is, I think, a cancer that eats at the heart of Christianity."[248]. To Crosson, the supernatural is the "beating heart of the natural" and therefore manifestations of God are like the metanarratives of the postmodernists created by communities to legitimize their belief structures. Subtract the worshippers from the equation and God disappears. Therefore, when Crosson is asked whether God existed during the Jurassic age, before humans existed, Crosson says that is a "meaningless question"[249]. Craig pushes the issue with Crosson in the debate:

> *"**Craig**: But surely that's not a meaningless question. It's a factual question. Was there a being who was the Creator and Sustainer of the universe during that period of time when no human beings existed? It seems to me that in your view you'd have to say no.*

> ***Crossan**: Well, I would probably prefer to say no because what you're doing is trying to put yourself in the position of God and ask, 'How is God apart from revelation? How is God apart from faith?' I don't know how you can do that. You can do it, I suppose, but I don't know if it really has any point."*

The postmodernist approach allows Biblical scholars such as Crosson to ostensibly accept the "validity" of multiple religions, not because they are true, but because they serve a purpose for the affected religious community. In reality, the postmodernist approach tends to delegitimize all theistic religions[250].

Although Jewish readers may think to themselves that the Jesus Seminar is Christianity's problem, I would remind them of Ramban's commentary to Genesis 1:1, to the effect that whoever does not believe that God created the universe and all that exists (i.e., believes that the universe always existed and was not itself created), does not share in the Torah. The postmodernist approach of Crosson and the Jesus Seminar can be seen also in promoters of "humanistic Judaism" who do not necessarily believe in the God of Israel, but support the culture, ethics and customs of the Jewish people - such as the Society for Humanistic Judaism[251] and the Congress of Secular Jewish Organizations[252]. The result of the efforts of the Jesus Seminar and promoters of "humanistic Judaism" (whether intended or not) may be the same - the de-legitimization of Judaism and Christianity. These issues are also not restricted to scholarly debates. The attack on theistic religion as an objective, unifying worldview is evident throughout our postmodernist culture, in literature, in film, on television and in the universities.

Focus Group Research

Some intriguing research has been conducted by Cultural Insights, Inc. for a number of Evangelical Christian groups in order to determine how best to witness to the unchurched and to less active Christians. Cultural Insights ran a number of focus groups around the United States with men and women in the 20-55 year age group. The participants in the groups were asked questions about their faith beliefs, but were also asked to pick out pictures from a large collection of photographs which represented their answers. This technique was used to try to minimize the participants' providing consciously screened "politically correct" answers.

The fascinating result of the focus groups was the discovery that many of the focus group participants viewed nature as the face or identity of God and viewed happiness as having the financial means to be isolated in nature (either alone or with close family). A diminished sense of community was found; instead, the participants viewed themselves as victims to a large extent. A certain level of mistrust of others was found, especially in the younger participants, who felt comfortable only in groups of people like themselves. The younger participants also did not like to see judgments of "right" or "wrong" being made by others. Also of note was the group's affinity to the Holy Spirit more than to God, with the Holy Spirit being seen as permeating nature and as providing inner peace. Little or no understanding was found as to the distinctions between God, Jesus and the Holy Spirit. Personal spiritual relationships were seen as possible with Jesus (God as "Provider"-the human God, concerned with human physical needs) and the Holy Spirit (God as "Caretaker"- the spirit which nurtures), but God Himself (God as "Creator") was seen as distant and judgmental.

When the Crosson/Jesus Seminar worldview is superimposed onto the Cultural Insights focus group results, the result appears to be that if Christians do not understand the Temple Judaism out of which Christianity grew, do not appreciate the creeds which first defined the Christian faith (Nicene creed, etc.), they will not view themselves as belonging to an historical "community of faith". They will forget that this is a community of faith which stretches back 4,000 years, where God intervened directly on the human plane to enter into a covenant with Abraham, bring the Israelites out of Egypt and bestow the Torah on them and then gave Jesus to die "as a ransom for others" - the Gentiles.

These Christians "who do not know their right hand from their left" (like the inhabitants of Nineveh) then may view God merely as a passive supernatural spirit that permeates nature and offers inner peace to believers of various faiths, but does not intervene directly in their lives. The danger of progressing from doctrinal ignorance and laxity to pagan pantheism appears to have been a topic of some controversy at the seventh assembly of the World Council of Churches in 1991, where some representatives issued a critical statement:

"...some people tend to affirm with very great ease the presence of the Holy Spirit in many movements and developments without discrimination...Our tradition is rich in respect for local and national cultures, but we find it impossible to invoke the spirits of 'earth, air, water and sea creatures.'"[253].

The concept of a passive God permeating nature runs counter to how God described Himself to Moses, as "I am that I am", which Rashi interprets to mean:

"I shall be with them in this suffering, I who will be with them in the servitude of other

kingdoms."[254].

And as one story recounts:

"A Hassidic rabbi (Hassidism is a mystical form of Judaism originating in eighteenth-century Eastern Europe) once asked a group of students, 'Where does God dwell?' Thinking the answer quite obvious, one of them called out, 'God is everywhere, of course!' Disagreeing with the answer, the rabbi said, 'God dwells wherever people let him in.'"[255].

The point of the above is that God is not a passive supernatural force permeating nature, but our God who is active throughout history and in our individual lives, but only to the extent we let Him in. As Matis Weinberg has written:

"Nature proclaims no specific directions, no teleological mechanism for Creation and evolution. Nature's dynamics and beauty are movingly impersonal, poignantly reminding us that we are visitors to a panorama of Life. Nature simply is. That is why, for all its fabulous galaxies and stunning mountains, for all its intricacies of atomic structure and mind-bending mathematics, Nature is not where the Presence is to be found. God is to be found holding the hand of the sick child, wiping the brow of the old woman struggling for breath, breathing the breath of life into an individual. This is not some maudlin sentiment, but a strict definition: the Presence exists only within relationship, within the sanctity of the individual."[256]

A disturbing result of the social trend toward belief in a passive God are Jews who derive their identity as Jews from the concept of ethnicity and shared cultural customs rather than from their religion - where a Tikkun magazine subscription and liberal politics is the badge of Jewishness rather than forming a *Minyan* at morning *Shacharit* service. The Jewish people are rightly proud of their history of social activism and healing the world ("*Tikkun Olam*") and it is true that familiarity with Yiddish and other uniquely Jewish cultural indicators can be important to one's identity as a Jew. But as has been noted by Rabbi Carol Harris-Shapiro[257], while "Jews for Jesus" have been spurned by the Jewish religious community (and correctly so in my personal view), secular Judaism has not been so forcefully rejected:

"When a Secular Humanistic congregation attempted to join the Union of American Hebrew Congregations (UAHC), it became a hotly debated issue among the Reform rabbinate, some of whose members pointed out that the Reform movement hardly required a creedal statement or belief in a supernatural God for membership (Cohn 1992; D. Friedman 1992). While the bid for membership ultimately failed in 1994

(Edelstein 1994, 63), the willingness of even a minority of Reform rabbis and congregations to accept a secular Jewish congregation within their ranks is instructive. Judaism historically has been a praxis-centered religion, with some latitude on theological beliefs; today, this accepted latitude appears to include disbelief as well. ***Ethnicity and social customs cannot be the ultimate bulwark to protect Judaism and the nation of Israel***...*As a rabbi, I seek some way of intelligently drawing the boundaries of Judaism and Jewishness, to respond to the challenge that Messianic Judaism represents to the Jewish community...**A continued identity based on a loose ethnic configuration and habitual custom, while it has served us well thus far in the United States, will not provide the motive energy to engage the next generation.** It is high time that together we figured out who we are."* [emphasis added]

In this postmodernist age, religions are being delegitimized and secularized by the popular culture and mixed ethnicity is becoming more prevalent. My own ancestry includes both Christians and Jews, ranging from Samuel Maycocke, who was an Anglican minister at the Jamestowne Colony in Virginia, to Jacob Simpson, an Orthodox Jew who immigrated to South Carolina from Napoleonic France and belonged to the Kahal Kadosh Beth Elohim synagogue in Charleston, South Carolina. Mixed ethnicity existed in the past and will occur more frequently in the future. Judaism should involve more than ethnic affinity. The devout Jew accepts the yoke of belief in the *Shema* and follows the commandments of the Torah in his or her everyday life, whether understood as being comprised of 613 Mitzvot, the thirteen principles of faith as set forth by Maimonides, or otherwise[258]. The devout Jew thereby acts as a benchmark and reminder of the "words of fire" of the Torah and the original covenant of God with Israel, through which a place in the world to come is merited.

The counterpart to the "humanistic" secular Jew is the secular Christian who believes that Christianity can be summed up simply as "God is love", reducing faith to the worldview of a social worker. Caring for the sick and elderly, feeding the hungry, visiting those in prison and promoting other social goals such as cleaning up the environment are all noble causes, but one can be an atheist and still support those causes. Belief in Jesus involves more than just "good works". Some Christian denominations believe that Christians are saved by their faith alone, with good works flowing automatically, just as fruit can be found on a healthy tree. To some Christians, good works are the outward and visible sign of an inward and spiritual grace. Other Christian denominations believe that good works and faith are both essential to salvation. Some Christians adhere to the Nicene Creed and other Church creeds, while others do not follow specific creeds. In any case, the devout Christian models his or her everyday life and actions after the life of Jesus, in the belief that salvation and a place in Heaven comes through following Jesus and the grace of God. The devout Christian (whatever the denomination) therefore serves as a benchmark and reminder of the "living waters" that Jesus offered his disciples, if they would die to their old life and be "reborn" in him.

Christians need to think of themselves as adopted sons of Joseph, just as Jesus was Joseph's adopted son. This concept is presented at the very beginning of the New Testament, where Joseph's lineage going back to David and Abraham is set forth in the first sixteen verses. Since Jesus was not conceived by Joseph, the only purpose for devoting the very first words in the New Testament to Joseph's lineage would be that early Christians believed in the importance and significance of Jesus being an adopted son of Joseph. Some readers may assume that Matthew set forth the genealogy solely in order to place Jesus within the Davidic line so as to identify Jesus as the Jewish Messiah (who devout Jews believe will be a descendant of King David), but this would be illogical since Joseph was not Jesus' biological father and in that case, Matthew could have stopped the listing of ancestors when King David was reached. Matthew also could have continued past Abraham to Adam, but he stopped at Abraham, the patriarch who was born the son of an idol-worshipper, but who smashed the idols of his father Terach and who was the first to worship the one God.

The point I believe Matthew is making is that just as Abraham rejected idol-worship and came to the one God later in life, so could Gentiles who repent of their pagan beliefs and who are "reborn" in Jesus, the adopted son of Joseph. Even the name of Joseph (Yosef in Hebrew, meaning "increase") is appropriate to this concept. As is noted in Genesis 30:24, Rachel named her son Yosef so that God would give her another son. Jesus ("Yeshua, meaning "salvation"), the son of Mary and the adopted son of Yosef, "increased" the number of followers of the God of Israel by "adopting" the repentant Gentiles and giving them the "living water" of faith in the God of Israel for their salvation. And as Marvin Wilson has noted[259]:

> "...Paul says that 'those who believe are children of Abraham' (Gal. 3:7); indeed, through faith, 'Abraham is the father of us all' (Rom. 4:16)...the New Testament also indicates that gentile believers - those who are spiritual rather than lineal descendants of Abraham - likewise share in this Abrahamic kinship (cf. Gal. 3:8). Indeed, all Christians find their origin in Abraham the Hebrew, for, as Paul states, 'If you belong in Christ, then you are Abraham's seed' (Gal. 3:19). The biblical phrase 'our father Abraham' (John 8:53; Acts 7:2) thus expresses the family relationship that every person of faith has with the 'man of faith' (Gal. 3:9)."

One last result of the Cultural Insights focus groups bears examination, moreover. When the participants were asked what questions they would ask God if given 24 hours to ask Him any question, the topic which was most important to all age groups, and to both men and women, was whether there was truly a resurrection after death and what it would be like. The Crosson/Jesus Seminar and "humanistic Judaism" approaches are inherently flawed since they offer no real assurance that there is any real meaning to life or that a virtuous life on earth will be rewarded with salvation in an afterlife. This presents an opportunity for both Judaism and Christianity in their mission to be "a light to the nations", for both religions stress the importance of the world to come as the reward for the faithful.

Ultimately, the choice between postmodern cynicism and theistic belief is the choice between the life of Esau and the life of Jacob. As one Jewish Midrash described the day Esau sold his religious birthright to Jacob:

"When Eisav came in that day, he found Ya'akov standing over the stove cooking lentil stew, eyes tearing from the smoke. Said Eisav to him, 'The rest of the world grabs any available food and you take the trouble to cook lentil stew?' Said Ya'akov to him, 'If we aren't willing to invest in the future, how can we work towards the day when the just are rewarded?' Said Eisav, 'You really believe in this Olam Haba [world to come] business? You think the dead will live again?' Said Ya'akov, 'If that's your attitude, what do you need this bechora [birthright] for anyway? Sell me today...'"[260] [explanatory text added in italics]

Creedal Faith

I have not distinguished between Christian denominations in this book and have relied more on Roman Catholic source materials for the various Church creeds quoted, since those creeds were adopted closer in time to the first century Christian church. I recognize that many of the Protestant Christian denominations have adopted their own creeds which may differ from the early Roman Catholic and Anglican Community creeds[261] and that some Protestant denominations have dispensed with creeds altogether. I have relied on Rabbinic sources from the first century and later periods to explain earlier texts and have not distinguished between different denominations of Judaism. I recognize, however, that Judaism, like Christianity, has also been evolving over the centuries due to the ongoing revelation of God in the world.

For example, beliefs in the resurrection of the body have evolved through the centuries[262]. Orthodox Jews today generally believe in the concept of the resurrection of the body, but Reform Judaism has generally rejected that belief in favor of belief in the immortality of the soul. Reform Judaism also has generally eliminated prayers from its liturgy which call for the restoration of the Temple (which would be the Third Temple) and its sacrifices.[263] Similar differences in beliefs with respect to the resurrection of the body can be found within Christian denominations today as well. No total harmonization of beliefs can be accomplished between Judaism and Christianity or even among various Christian denominations or among Orthodox,

Conservative, Reform or Reconstructionist Judaism.

Instead of attempting harmonization between varied belief systems which have evolved considerably through the centuries, I have simply tried to establish that early Rabbinic Judaism and first century Christianity may have been more closely related with respect to their theological worldviews than may popularly be thought the case. I have tried to establish for Jewish readers that Christianity may serve an important goal of Judaism, by bringing the Gentiles of many nations to the God of Israel, so that both Judaism and Christianity may serve the God of Israel as a "light unto the nations". I also have tried to establish for Christian readers that by learning about Judaism - *by drawing nearer to the fire of the Torah* - Christians can develop a more nuanced and deeper understanding of the answer to the question "What would Jesus do?", because Jesus unquestionably was of the Jews[264]. Hopefully this book may also persuade supersessionist Christians that aggressively proselytizing to the Jewish community (as versus having an open, but respectful dialogue with the Jewish community) is not God's will, since His covenant with the Jews is eternally valid.

Ecumenical Considerations

In "Song of Ascents", "Sign of Jonah" and "Dominion", I have attempted to create paradigms for a renewed Jewish-Christian dialogue. I hope that devout Jews and devout Christians will recognize this kinship and see that they face equal threats from the secular, postmodernist world and should face that threat together. The Vatican Declaration "*Nostra Aetate*", the recent Vatican reflection document "*The Gifts and the Calling of God are Irrevocable (Rom 11:29): A Reflection on Theological Questions Pertaining to Catholic Jewish Relations on the Occasion of the 50th Anniversary of 'Nostra Aetate (No. 4)'*"and the *Orthodox Rabbinic Statement on Christianity: To Do the Will of Our Father in Heaven - Toward a Partnership between Jews and Christians*" represent an historic next step in recognizing this kinship. As the "*Orthodox Rabbinic Statement on Christianity*" states:

> "*After nearly two millennia of mutual hostility and alienation, we Orthodox Rabbis who lead communities, institutions and seminaries in Israel, the United States and Europe recognize the historic opportunity now before us. We seek to do the will of our Father in Heaven by accepting the hand offered to us by our Christian brothers and sisters...Nostra Aetate and the later official Church documents it inspired unequivocally reject any form of anti- Semitism, affirm the eternal Covenant between G-d and the Jewish people, reject deicide and stress the unique relationship between Christians and Jews, who were called 'our elder brothers' by Pope John Paul II and 'our fathers in faith' by Pope Benedict XVI...Both Jews and Christians have a common covenantal mission to perfect the world under the sovereignty of the Almighty, so that all humanity will call on His name...."*

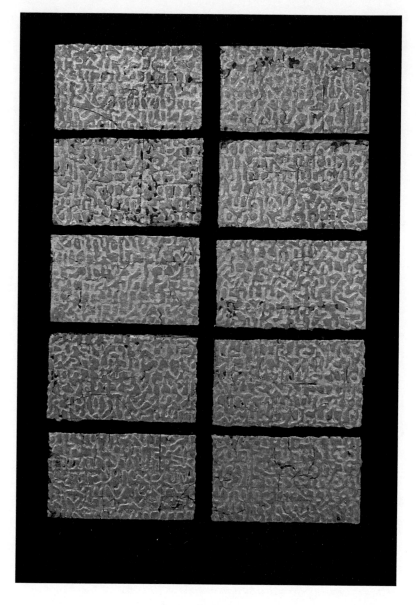

"Decalogue"

This "Ten Commandments" piece was constructed of ten gilded collagraph sheaves floating above the surface of the paper. The entire Decalogue was written on a Masonite plate, printed using an etching press in a sienna color on a heavy paper, then gilded and surfaced with iridescent craypas to give a luminous quality to the image. Collagraph mixed media 2003 30"x22"- Sandra Bowden

Endnotes

1 See H. Bialik and Y. Ravnitzky, The Book of Legends: Sefer Ha-Aggadah: Legends From the Talmud and Midrash (Schocken Books 1992) at p. 393 n.41.

2 See H. Bialik and Y. Ravnitzky, The Book of Legends - Sefer Ha-Aggadah: Legends from the Talmud and Midrash (Schocken Books 1992) at p. 485 n. 144.

3 See John Gardner and Francesca Gardner, Quotations of Wit and Wisdom (W. W. Norton 1998) at pg. 98.

4 See H. Bialik and Y. Ravnitzky, The Book of Legends - Sefer Ha-Aggadah: Legends from the Talmud and Midrash (Schocken Books 1992) at p. 403 n. 12.

5 See Menahem Mansoor, Biblical Hebrew: Step by Step (vol. 1) (Baker Book House 1993) at pg. 33.

6 See J. Charlesworth, "Christians and Jews in the First Six Centuries", in Hershel Shanks, Christianity and Rabbinic Judaism: A Parallel History of Their Origins and Early Development (Biblical Archaeology Society 1982) at pg. 306.

7 See M. Wise, M. Abegg, Jr., and E. Cook, The Dead Sea Scrolls: A New Translation (HarperSanFrancisco 1996) ("Wise/Abegg/Cook") at pg. 34.

8 See, e.g., Hershel Shanks, Understanding the Dead Sea Scrolls (Random House 1992) at p. 41.

9 See Wise/Abegg/Cook at pg. 34.

10 See Rabbi Elyse Goldstein, ReVisions: Seeing Torah Through a Feminist Lens (Jewish Lights Publishing 1998) at p. 182.

11 See Jay Greenspan, Hebrew Calligraphy (Schocken Books 1981) at p. xvii.

12 See Wise/Abegg/Cook at pg. 91.

13 Rev. Fleming Rutledge highlights this image from the Psalms - of God being enthroned on the praises of Israel - in her book, The Bible and The New York Times (Wm. B. Eerdmans Pub. 1998) (see pg. 24). Her sermon "The Meeting of the Lord" (pp. 74-79), recounting the presentation of Jesus at the Temple as an infant, inspired my piece in this book entitled "Song of Ascents".

14 See H. Bialik and Y. Ravnitzky, The Book of Legends: Sefer Ha-Aggadah - Legends From the Talmud and Midrash (Schocken Books 1992) at pg. 701 n. 132, where it states "The Holy One hates him who says one thing in his mouth and another in his heart."; see also pg. 700 n. 110: "A company of liars cannot receive the presence".

15 See Rabbi Adin Steinsaltz, The Talmud: A Reference Guide (Random House 1989) at pg. 175.

16 See L. Schlesinger and Rabbi S. Vogel, The Ten Commandments: The Significance of God's Laws in Everyday Life (HarperCollins 1998) at pg. 241.

17 Quoted in Geza Vermes, Jesus the Jew: A Historian's Reading of the Gospels (Fortress Press

1973) at pg. 10.

18 See A. Kolatch, <u>This is the Torah</u> (Jonathan David Publishers, Inc. 1994) at pp. 7-11.

19 A. Bonchek, <u>What's Bothering Rashi?: A Guide to In-Depth Analysis of his Torah Commentary- Shemos [Exodus]</u>(Feldheim Publishers 1999) at pg. 123.

20 See, e.g., Stefan Reif, "Aspects of the Jewish Contribution to Biblical Interpretation", in John Barton (ed.), <u>The Cambridge Companion to Biblical Interpretation</u> (Cambridge University Press 1998) at pg. 143.

21 For a fuller discussion of this point, see footnote 218 to the piece in this book entitled "Sign of Jonah", which describes the key references to the Temple sacrificial offerings in the modern-day Synagogue liturgy and explains why certain prayers are not recited at specific services due to their connection to Temple practices.

22 Neil Gillman, "Shabbat Zachor/Vayikra: Temple Sacrifices", in <u>The Jewish Week</u>, March 17, 2000.

23 It is also important to note that sin (Chatas) and guilt (Asham) offerings were a key part of the Temple sacrifices and that the Rabbis who developed what is now the modern-day Synagogue prayer service structure believed that "forgiveness from sin can be achieved by recitation of the order of sacrifices and that this activity is equivalent to offering the sacrifices themselves" (see Stephen Schach, <u>The Structure of the Siddur</u> [Prayer Book] (Jason Aronson 1996) at pg. 230). Accordingly, although some readers might think that rabbinic Judaism places little emphasis on sin except on Yom Kippur, the weekly recitations by the worshippers of the description of the Temple sin and guilt offerings in Synagogue services is deemed the equivalent of their making sin and guilt offerings in the Second Temple. Also, the Tachanun (supplication) prayer, which is traditionally recited after the weekday Amidah, during the Synagogue Morning Service and Afternoon Service, is an express confession of sin and prayer for forgiveness (Rachum v'chanun, chatati l'fanecha...v'kabel tachanunai: O merciful and gracious God, I have sinned before You... accept my supplications). The short version of the Tachanun, which is read on weekdays during the Afternoon Service and during the weekday Morning Service (except on Mondays and Thursdays when the long Tachanun is recited), concludes with a prayer for forgiveness (Va-anachnu lo nedah mah na-aseh: We do not know what to do), which includes biblical verses pleading for salvation and forgiveness from sin. If the Tachanun is recited in a room with an Ark containing a Torah scroll, the worshipper traditionally recites Psalm 6:2-11, the second part of the Tachanun (Adonai, al b'apcha tochicheni: O Lord, do not punish me in Your anger) with the forehead resting on the arm (see Schach, supra, at pp. 135-136). Finally, the Additional Service in Synagogues contains the Hoshanot ("please save") prayers, which includes the E-eroch shu-i and El l'mosha- ot Hoshana prayers dealing with repentance and the God who saves.(see Schach, supra, at pg. 241).

24 RSV Bible. The circumstances surrounding Simeon's meeting of Mary, Joseph and Jesus at the Temple is described in Luke 2:21-28:

94

"And at the end of the eight days, when he was circumcised, he was called Jesus, the name given by the angel before he was conceived in the womb. And when the time came for their purification according to the law of Moses, they brought him up to Jerusalem to present him to the Lord (as it is written in the law of the Lord, 'Every male that opens the womb shall be called holy to the Lord') and to offer a sacrifice according to what is said in the law of the Lord, 'a pair of turtledoves, or two young pigeons.' Now there was a man in Jerusalem, whose name was Simeon, and this man was righteous and devout, looking for the consolation of Israel, and the Holy Spirit was upon him. And it had been revealed to him by the Holy Spirit that he should not see death before he had seen the Lord's Christ. And inspired by the Spirit he came into the temple; and when the parents brought in the child Jesus, to do for him according to the custom of the law, he took him up in his arms and blessed God...": Luke 2:25-28.

25 Sinai Tanakh [all quotes from Psalms 120-134 in the "Song of Ascents: Psalms of Degrees for the Pilgrimage to Jerusalem" are from the Sinai Tanakh]

26 "In the eighth century BC the prophet Isaiah wrote of the 'District [Gelil] of Gentiles', the phrase from which the name Galilee derives": see Geza Vermes, Jesus the Jew: A Historian's Reading of the Gospels (Fortress Press 1973) at pg. 44.

27 "Tuma'a" in Hebrew.

28 See Rabbi Adin Steinsaltz, The Talmud: A Reference Guide (Random House 1989) at pg. 199.

29 See Exodus 34:24.

30 See H. Bialik and Y. Ravnitzky, The Book of Legends - Sefer Ha-Aggadah: Legends from the Talmud and Midrash (Schocken Books 1992) at pg. 160 n. 3; see also Talmud, Tractate Yoma (Day of Atonement) 12a.

31 See A. Edersheim, The Temple: Its Ministry and Services as they Were at the Time of Jesus Christ (Kregel Publications 1997) at pg. 243.

32 See H. Bialik and Y. Ravnitzky, The Book of Legends - Sefer Ha-Aggadah: Legends From the Talmud and Midrash (Schocken Books 1992) at pg. 175 n. 63.

33 "Formally, the Sabbath commenced at sunset on Friday, the day being reckoned by the Hebrews from sunset to sunset...The approach of the Sabbath, and then its actual commencement, were announced by threefold blasts from the priests' trumpets. The first three blasts were drawn ... about the ninth hour, that is, about three P.M. on Friday...When the priests for the first time sounded their trumpets, all business was to cease, and every kind of work to be stopped. Next the Sabbath-lamp, of which even heathen writers knew, was lit, and the festive garments put on. A second time the priests drew a threefold blast, to indicate the Sabbath had actually begun": See A. Edersheim, The Temple: Its Ministry and Services as they were at the

<u>Time</u> <u>of</u> <u>Jesus</u> <u>Christ</u> (Kregel Publications 1997) at pg. 122. A tablet has been discovered which is believed to have once been part of the Second Temple structure, upon which tablet is inscribed in Hebrew the words "To the house of trumpeting", presumably the location in the southwest corner of the Temple where the Priest announced the Sabbath with three blasts of a trumpet (see Edersheim, ibid., at pp. 127 and 201); see also M Ben-Dov, M. Naor and Z. Aner, <u>The</u> <u>Western</u> <u>Wall</u> (Ministry of Defence-Publishing House 1987) at pg. 49, where it is noted that the high tower for the sounding of the Shabbat shofar looked out over the lower market of Jerusalem consisting of hundreds of shops on both sides of a main road which ran along the length of the Tyropoeon Valley reaching the Siloam Pool. The authors speculate that the inscription originally read "For the place of sounding for...the announcement of the Sabbath."

34 See Rabbi H. Donin, <u>To</u> <u>Pray</u> <u>as</u> <u>a</u> <u>Jew</u> (BasicBooks 1980) at pg. 11.

35 See R. Isaacs, <u>Jewish</u> <u>Music:</u> <u>Its</u> <u>History,</u> <u>People,</u> <u>and</u> <u>Song</u> (Jason Aaronson 1997) at pg. 1; see also A. Edersheim, <u>The</u> <u>Temple:</u> <u>Its</u> <u>Ministry</u> <u>and</u> <u>Services</u> <u>As</u> <u>They</u> <u>Were</u> <u>at</u> <u>the</u> <u>Time</u> <u>of</u> <u>Jesus</u> <u>Christ</u> (Kregel Publications 1997) at pg. 126; see also A. Kolatch, <u>This</u> <u>is</u> <u>the</u> <u>Torah</u> (Jonathan David Publishers 1998) at pg. 113. According to the traditions of the Masoretes, who designed the format of the Torah, the Song at the Sea (Exodus 15:1-19) is written by scribes (Soferim) so that it creates the effect of a wall of water like a brick wall. The song is to be written in thirty lines, with the first line written out full. The second line is divided into three written sections, with open space in between. The third line has two written sections, with white space in between. This pattern is continued for the balance of the thirty lines, creating the visual effect of a wall of water. Similarly, the Song of Moses is traditionally written in seventy lines, with each line having an open space in the middle of it, evoking the two walls of water, between which the Israelites passed (see A. Kolatch, <u>This</u> <u>is the</u> <u>Torah</u> (Jonathan David Publishers 1998) at pg. 112).

36 Sinai Tanakh

37 See Josephus, <u>The</u> <u>Jewish</u> <u>War</u> (Penguin Classics 1981) at pg. 361.

38 See M. Strassfeld, <u>The</u> <u>Jewish</u> <u>Holidays:</u> <u>A</u> <u>Guide</u> <u>and</u> <u>Commentary</u> (Harper & Row 1985) at pg. 69.

39 See <u>Encyclopedia</u> <u>Judaica</u>, under the entry for "Sukkot"; see also Talmud, Tractate Sotah 7:8; Deuteronomy 31:10-11

40 One ivory pomegranate with six petals as described was found and is believed to be the only known relic from Solomon's Temple in Jerusalem (see I. Fischof, <u>Jewish</u> <u>Art</u> <u>Masterpieces</u> <u>From</u> <u>the</u> <u>Israel</u> <u>Museum</u> (HLA Associates 1994) at pg. 18. Although the one ivory pomegranate has a small rounded hole in its bottom suggesting that it has been mounted on a rod, no one knows its actual use in the Temple. I have taken literary license in imagining that it had a mate, that the two pomegranates were used as finials on the Temple Torah scroll rods around which the scroll was wrapped, and that the twelve petals on the two pomegranates represented the twelve tribes.

41 Exodus 19:2 states "And Israel encamped there [*at the foot of Sinai*]...." [explanatory note added in italics], but uses the singular form for Israel, as if it read "And he encamped there"

rather than "And they encamped there." Accordingly, Rashi interprets this to mean that the Israelites encamped there as one man, with one heart: See Rabbi Shimon Finkelman, Shavuos - Its Observance, Laws and Significance (Mesorah Publications 1995) at pg. 85.

42 See Rabbi Adin Steinsaltz, The Talmud: A Reference Guide (Random House 1989) at pg. 239.

43 See H. Bialik and Y. Ravnitzky, The Book of Legends - Sefer Ha-Aggadah: Legends From the Talmud and Midrash (Schocken Books 1992) at pg. 183 notes 85-89.

44 Talmud, Tractate Middot (Measurements) 2:5.

45 See Rabbi Adin Steinsaltz, The Talmud: A Reference Guide (Random House 1989) at pp. 276-277 for a drawing of the altar and the plan of the Temple; see also, Josephus, The Jewish War (Penguin Classics 1981) at pg. 492.

46 See Edersheim, ibid. at pg. 60.

47 I. Levanoni, The Temple: A Description of the Second Temple According to the Rambam (Brit Chalom Editions 1997) at pg. 47.

48 I. Levanoni, The Temple: A Description of the Second Temple According to the Rambam (Brit Chalom Editions 1997) at pg. 49.

49 I. Levanoni, The Temple: A Description of the Second Temple According to the Rambam (Brit Chalom Editions 1997) at pg. 48.

50 Query whether this is a reference to an earlier priestly sect akin to the Qumran community, which followed a solar calendar, rather than the lunar calendar followed by the Second Temple priests?

51 See Psalm 128:5-6; see also H. Bialik and Y. Ravnitzky, The Book of Legends- Sefer Ha-Aggadah: Legends from the Talmud and the Midrash (Schocken Books 1992) at pg. 183 n.85.

52 See Zechariah 14:16.

53 See Talmud, Tractate Kelim (vessels) 17:9; Talmud, Tractate Menachot (Meal Offerings) 98a; Josephus, The Jewish War (Penguin Classics 1981) at pg. 302.

54 M Ben-Dov, M. Naor and Z. Aner, The Western Wall (Ministry of Defence-Publishing House 1987) at pg. 48.

55 See Josephus, The Jewish War (Penguin Classics 1981) at pg. 302.

56 See A. Edersheim, The Temple: Its Ministry and Services as They Were at the Time of Jesus Christ (Kregel Publications 1997) at pg. 18.

57 See A. Edersheim, The Temple: Its Ministry and Services as They Were at the Time of Jesus Christ (Kregel Publications 1997) at pg. 18.

58 see Talmud, Tractate Bava Batra (Last Gate) 4a, part of Talmud, Tractate Nezikin (Damages).

59 See Josephus, The Jewish War (Penguin Classics 1981) at pg. 492.

60 Talmud, Tractate Middoth (Measurements) 1b.

61 Talmud, Tractate Middoth (Measurements) 1:3

62 See Leviticus 7:12-13.

63 See Rabbi H. Donin, To Pray as a Jew (BasicBooks 1980) at pg. 175.

64 To this day, many Orthodox Jews will not set foot upon the Temple Mount, for fear that they might accidentally step upon the area above the former Holy of Holies. For a fascinating exploration of where the sacrificial altar and the Holy of Holies were located on the Temple Mount, see David Jacobson, "Sacred Geometry: Unlocking the Secret of the Temple Mount - Part 1", Biblical Archaeology Review (July/August 1999) at pg. 42; David Jacobson, "Sacred Geometry: Unlocking the Secret of the Temple Mount - Part 2", Biblical Archaeology Review (September/October 1999) at pg. 54.

65 See Talmud, Tractate Shekalim (Shekels) 2:1, 6:1

66 See Talmud, Tractate Yoma (Day of Atonement) 55b; A. Edersheim, The Temple: Its Ministry and Services as they Were at the Time of Jesus Christ (Kregel Publications 1997) at pg.40.

67 Talmud, Tractate Yoma (Day of Atonement) 55a.

68 The mezuzah was on the Nicanor gate because the apartment of the High Priest was near to it (see Talmud, Tractate Yoma (Day of Atonement) 11a).

69 see H. Bialik and Y. Ravnitzky, The Book of Legends- Sefer Ha-Aggadah: Legends from the Talmud and the Midrash (Schocken Books 1992) at pg. 160 n.5; see also Talmud, Tractate Yoma (Day of Atonement) 38a.

70 See H. Bialik and Y. Ravnitzky, The Book of Legends- Sefer Ha-Aggadah: Legends from the Talmud and the Midrash (Schocken Books 1992) at pg. 572 n.317; see also Talmud, Tractate Shabbat (Sabbath) 152b.

71 See Rabbi Adin Steinsaltz, The Talmud: A Reference Guide (Random House 1989) at pg. 185.

72 See Talmud, Tractate Yoma (Day of Atonement) 33a.

73 See Josephus, The Jewish War (Penguin Classics 1981) at pg. 304.

74 See Rabbi Adin Steinsaltz, The Talmud: A Reference Guide (Random House 1989) at pg. 252.

75 Talmud, Tractate Yoma (Day of Atonement) 21b.

76 See Josephus, The Jewish War (Penguin Books 1981) at pg. 304.

77 See Mishne Torah, Hilchot Beit Habehira, 2:1:2 "It is a tradition held by all that the place upon which David and Shelomo built the altar on the threshing floor of Aravnah is the very same place where Avraham built his altar...", quoted in Matis Weinberg, FrameWorks: Shemot [Exodus] (Foundation for Jewish Publications 1999) at pg. 253.

78 See Talmud, Tractate Yoma (Day of Atonement) 55b.

79 See A. Edersheim, The Temple: Its Ministry and Services As They Were at the Time of Jesus Christ (Kregel Publications 1997) at pg. 227; See Rabbi Adin Steinsaltz, The Talmud: A Reference Guide (Random House 1989) at pg. 195.

80 See M Ben-Dov, M. Naor and Z. Aner, The Western Wall (Ministry of Defence-Publishing

House 1987) at pg. 42.

81 See Deuteronomy 8:8; see also M Ben-Dov, M. Naor and Z. Aner, The Western Wall (Ministry of Defence - Publishing House 1987) at pp. 24, 29.

82 Exodus 23:19 and 34:26.

83 See Talmud, Tractate Bikkurim (First Fruit) 1, 6, 9.

84 Although the festival of Bikkurim (First Fruits) no longer is celebrated, Jews stand up in the presence of a brit (circumcision) and a funeral procession, two customs whose origins can be found in the ceremony of bringing up the Bikkurim: see Bartinura on Mishna Bikkurim 3:3. The Mikra Bikkurim is also recited as part of the Pesach Seder.

85 See H. Bialik and Y. Ravnitzky, The Book of Legends: Sefer Ha-Aggadah - Legends From the Talmud and Midrash (Schocken Books 1992) at pg. 177 n. 74.

86 See Rabbi Adin Steinsaltz, The Talmud: A Reference Guide (Random House 1989) at pg. 270.

87 The 22 X 33 inch limestone tablet was found in 1871 and reads in Greek as follows: "No stranger is to enter within the balustrade around the temple and enclosure; whoever is caught will be responsible to himself for his death, which will ensue." (see R. Backhouse, The Kregel Pictorial Guide to the Temple (Kregel Publications 1996) at pg. 12.

88 See Numbers 6:2-8.

89 See H. Bialik and Y. Ravnitzky, The Book of Legends- Sefer Ha-Aggadah: Legends from the Talmud and the Midrash (Schocken Books 1992) at pp. 161-162 n. 13 and pg. 162 n. 14.

90 See H. Bialik and Y. Ravnitzky, The Book of Legends- Sefer Ha-Aggadah: Legends from the Talmud and the Midrash (Schocken Books 1992) at pg. 162 n. 14.

91 See H. Bialik and Y. Ravnitzky, The Book of Legends- Sefer Ha-Aggadah: Legends from the Talmud and the Midrash (Schocken Books 1992) at pg. 161 n. 12.

92 I. Levanoni, The Temple: A Description of the Second Temple According to the Rambam (Brit Chalom Editions 1997) at pg. 22; See also Rabbi Adin Steinsaltz, The Talmud: A Reference Guide (Random House 1989) at pg. 168.

93 Tzara'as is not clinical leprosy, but the whiteness of skin evidencing a spiritual "leprosy" no longer seen in modern times, which was caused by any one of ten sins, with the most severe form being caused by "lashon hara" - an evil tongue - and which could appear on clothing and the walls of houses as well as on the skin; See Rabbi M. Weissman, The Midrash Says: The Book of Vayikra [Leviticus] (Benei Yakov Publications 1982) at pp. 121- 169).

94 See Leviticus 14:1-9; see also Rabbi Moshe Weissman, The Midrash Says: Vayikra [Leviticus] (Benei Yakov Publications 1982) at pg. 121.

95 See Talmud, Tractate Tamid (Daily Sacrifice) 30a, 30b.

96 See Talmud, Tractate Tamid (Daily Sacrifice) 32b; See Rabbi Adin Steinsaltz, The Talmud: A Reference Guide (Random House 1989) at pg. 173.

97 See A. Edersheim, ibid at p. 114.

98 See Talmud, Tractate Tamid (Daily Sacrifice) 33b.

99 See H. Bialik and Y. Ravnitzky, The Book of Legends- Sefer Ha-Aggadah: Legends from the Talmud and the Midrash (Schocken Books 1992) at pg. 163. n.3.

100 See Talmud, Tractate Talmud (Daily Sacrifice) 33b.

101 See Encyclopedia Judaica entry for "Tamid".

102 See Rabbi Adin Steinsaltz, The Talmud: A Reference Guide (Random House 1989) at pg. 188.

103 Talmud, Tractate Yoma (Day of Atonement) 25a.

104 For a more detailed description of the order of the sacrifices at the morning service, see Talmud, Tractate Yoma (Day of Atonement) 33a.

105 R. Isaacs, Jewish Music: Its History, People, and Song (Jason Aaronson 1997) at pp. 43-49.

106 See Talmud, Tractate Tamid (Daily Sacrifice) 33b.

107 The order of the Psalms during the weekly services were as follows [all quotes are from the Sinai Tanakh]:

First day of the week (Sunday): Psalm 24, "The earth is the Lord's", representing the first day of creation

Second day of the week (Monday): Psalm 48, "Great is the Lord, and greatly to be praised in the city of our God, in the mountain of his holiness", because God separated the waters from the waters on the second day, making the firmament

Third day of the week (Tuesday): Psalm 82, "God standeth in the congregation of the mighty; he judgeth among the judges", because God created the earth on the third day, on which are those to be judged

Fourth day of the week (Wednesday): Psalm 94, "O Lord God, to whom vengeance belongeth", because God will avenge Himself on those who worship the sun, moon or stars created on the fourth day

Fifth day of the week (Thursday): Psalm 81, "Sing aloud unto God our strength", because on the fifth day God created all manners of fish and other creatures who praise His name

Sixth day of the week (Friday): Psalm 93, "The Lord reigneth", because on that day God created man, cattle and the beasts of the earth and He finished the last of His works, over all of whom He reigns

Seventh day of the week (Saturday): Psalm 92, "It is a good thing to give thanks unto the

Lord", because the Sabbath is symbolic of the millennial kingdom when His glory would fill the earth with thanksgiving; See R. Isaacs, Jewish Music: Its History, People, and Song (Jason Aaronson 1997) at pp. 34-41; see also A. Edersheim, The Temple: Its Ministry and Services As They Were at the Time of Jesus Christ (Kregel Publications 1997) at pg. 116. [For reasons set forth in the commentary entitled "Sign of Jonah" in this book, I imagine that Jesus was presented on a Sunday, the first day of the week and therefore the Levites sang Psalm 24 at the Temple service on the day Jesus was presented]

108 "Selah" may have been an instruction to the Levites and worshippers to raise their voices (see R. Isaacs, Jewish Music: Its History, People, and Song (Jason Aaronson 1997) at pg. 32; others theorize that it may have been a liturgical response from the worshippers meaning "always" or "for eternity": see Encyclopedia Judaica under the entry for "Book of Psalms".

109 Sinai Tanakh

110 See Josephus, The Jewish War (Penguin Classics 1981) at pg. 305.

111 I. Levanoni, The Temple: A Description of the Second Temple According to the Rambam (Brit Chalom Editions 1997) at pg. 34.

112 See A. Eidersheim, ibid, at pg. 70-72.

113 See Rabbi Adin Steinsaltz, The Talmud: A Reference Guide (Random House 1989) at pg. 168.

114 See Talmud, Tractate Yoma (Day of Atonement) 18a.

115 See Talmud, Tractate Yoma (Day of Atonement) 31b; see also Menachem Oppen, The Yom Kippur Avodah (C.I.S. Publishers 1995) at pg. 23.

116 See Talmud, Tractate Yoma (Day of Atonement) 7a.

117 See Josephus, The Jewish War (Penguin Classics 1981) at pg. 305.

118 See Talmud, Tractate Yoma 73b n.8.

119 See Rabbi Moshe Weissman, What the Midrash Says: The Book of Sh'mos [Exodus] (Benei Yakov Publications 1980) at pg. 294; see also Wise/Abegg/Cook, Dead Sea Scrolls at pp. 178-179.

120 See Talmud, Tractate Tamid (Daily Sacrifices) 28b.

121 I. Levanoni, The Temple: A Description of the Second Temple According to the Rambam (Brit Chalom Editions 1997) at pg. 31; See Rabbi Adin Steinsaltz, The Talmud: A Reference Guide (Random House 1989) at pg. 191.

122 On holidays and on Rosh Hodesh, a prayer known as "Ya'aleh V'yavo" is added to the Retzei blessing, a part of the Amidah prayer (otherwise known as the Prayer of Eighteen Blessings) said in Temples and Synagogues throughout the world today. The Ya'aleh V'yavo prayer is a "synopsis of the event" (Talmud, Tractate Shabbos 24a), meaning a synopsis of the sequence of events occurring at the Second Temple when an offering was made: "Our God and God of our fathers, May there ascend (ya'aleh), come forward (yavo), draw near (yageea), appear (yei'ra-eh), be accepted (yeiratzeh), be heard (yishama), counted (yipaked) and remembered

101

(yiszkher) before Thee [o]ur remembrances...." (see Rabbi H. Donin, <u>To Pray as a Jew</u> (BasicBooks 1980) at pg. 132).

123 See Talmud, Tractate Middoth (Measurements) 35b; See Rabbi Adin Steinsaltz, <u>The Talmud: A Reference Guide</u> (Random House 1989) at pp. 190, 217, 229.

124 See Talmud, Tractate Yoma (Day of Atonement) 62b; see also Talmud, Tractate Tamid (Daily Sacrifice) 30b.

125 See Talmud, Tractate Tamid (Daily Sacrifice) 30b.

126 See Rabbi Adin Steinsaltz, <u>The Talmud: A Reference Guide</u> (Random House 1989) at pg. 191.

127 See Josephus, <u>The Jewish War</u> (Penguin Classics 1981) at pg. 304.

128 See Talmud, Tractate Tamid (Daily Sacrifice) 33b.

129 See Josephus, <u>The Jewish War</u> (Penguin Classics 1981) at pg. 304-305.

130 Talmud, Tractate Yoma (Day of Atonement) 19a.

131 See Rabbi Adin Steinsaltz, <u>The Talmud: A Reference Guide</u> (Random House 1989) at pg. 168.

132 I. Levanoni, <u>The Temple: A Description of the Second Temple According to the Rambam</u> (Brit Chalom Editions 1997) at pg. 37.

133 See A. Edersheim, ibid, at pp. 22, 222.

134 See Menachem Oppen, <u>The Yom Kippur Avodah</u> (C.I.S. Publishers 1995) at pg. 35. 135 See Leviticus 16:8,10, 26; Talmud, Tractate Yoma (Day of Atonement) 66a; see also Menachem Oppen, <u>The Yom Kippur Avodah</u> (C.I.S. Publishers 1995) at pg. 63.

136 Sinai Tanakh; See H. Bialik and Y. Ravnitzky, <u>The Book of Legends - Sefer Ha-Aggadah: Legends from the Talmud and Midrash</u> (Schocken Books 1992) at pg. 162 n. 16 and pp. 179-80 n. 75.

137 "Our masters taught: At one time, a strand of crimson wool would be tied on the outside of the entrance to the Porch [Ulam]. If it turned white, they rejoiced; if it did not turn white, they were sad and shamefaced. Then it was arranged to have it tied on the inside of the entrance to the Porch. But the people still managed to have a look at it, and if it became white, they rejoiced, but if it did not become white, they were sad and shamefaced. Then it was ordained to have one half of the strand tied to a rock and the other half tied between the horns of the he-goat that is sent away.": See H. Bialik and Y. Ravnitzky, <u>The Book of Legends - Sefer Ha-Aggadah: Legends from the Talmud and Midrash</u> (Schocken Books 1992) at pg. 181 n. 77; see also Menachem Oppen, <u>The Yom Kippur Avodah</u> (C.I.S. Publishers 1995) at pg. 92; see Talmud, Tactate Yoma (Day of Atonement) 67a.

138 See Leviticus 23:34.

139 See Matis Weinberg, <u>FrameWorks: Bereishit [Genesis]</u> (Foundation for Jewish Publications 1999) at pg. 30, quoting Rashi: "When the Most High gave nations their heritage and split up the sons of man, He set the definition of nations according to the number of the Children of Yisrael

(Devarim [*Deuteronomy*] 32:8) - [Paralleling the seventy individuals of Yisrael [*Jacob*] who went down to Egypt did 'He set the definitions of nations,' seventy languages. (-Rashi)]" [explanatory text added in italics].

140 See H. Bialik and Y. Ravnitzky, <u>The Book of Legends - Sefer Ha-Aggadah: Legends from the Talmud and Midrash</u> (Schocken Books 1992) at pg. 173 n. 58.

141 See Talmud, Tractate Sukkah (Booth) 4:5.

142 See Marvin Wilson, <u>Our Father Abraham: Jewish Roots of the Christian Faith</u> (Wm. Eerdmans Pub. Co. 1989) at pg. 215.

143 See, e.g., Matthew 24:1-2: "Jesus left the temple and was going away, when his disciples came to point out to him the buildings of the temple. But he answered them, 'You see all these, do you not? Truly, I say to you, there will not be left here one stone upon another, that will not be thrown down.'"

144 See Rabbi H. Donin, <u>To Pray as a Jew</u> (BasicBooks 1980) at pg. 11.

145 See H. Bialik and Y. Ravnitzky, <u>The Book of Legends -Sefer Ha-Aggadah: Legends From the Talmud and Midrash</u> (Schocken Books 1992) at pg. 183 n. 86

146 It was conjectured by some of the Jewish Sages that the Second Temple was destroyed because the inhabitants of Jerusalem conducted their affairs strictly by the Mosaic law, implying that not enough love and charity was shown by the Israelites to one another: see Rabbi Adin Steinsaltz, <u>The Talmud: A Reference Guide</u> (Random House 1989) at pg. 209. Others of the Jewish Sages theorized that "baseless hatred" (Sinat Chinam) between Jews (e.g., the denial of the grace and unique identity of one's fellow Jew) at the time was the root cause of the Second Temple's destruction: See Talmud, Tractate Yoma (Day of Atonement) 9a.

147 What sign might have been sought by Jesus' Jewish audience? Perhaps it was the password that occurred in every reference to redemption of the Israelites in the Torah, "Pacode yifcode" - God will rendezvous with you. As Matis Weinberg explains in his <u>FrameWorks: Shemot [Exodus]</u> (Foundation for Jewish Publications 1999) at pg.39, citing to Pirkei Rabbi Eliezer: 47:

> "*Pacode Yifcode...This code was passed from Avraham to Yitzhak, from Yitzhak to Ya'akov, and Ya'akov revealed this code of ge'ula [**redemption**] to Yosef: 'Pacode yifcode' -God will rendezvous with you (Bereishit 50:240). Then Yosef his son passed the code of ge'ula on to his brothers, and told them: 'Pacode yifcode' -God will rendezvous with you... (ibid. 50:25). Asher [**his brother**] passed the code to his own daughter, Serah. When Moshe and Aharon came to the elders of Yisrael and performed signs before them [**and said the code words**], they consulted with Serah, Asher's daughter...'Then it is he!' she exclaimed. 'That is the man who will redeem us from Egypt." [explanatory text added in bold]*

Matis Weinberg explains further that: "'Pacode' is a word loaded with intimations of faith and hope. It combines the connotations of 'remember', 'act upon', 'appointment', 'care' and 'tryst' to suggest a vision of ge'ula." Matis Weinberg also shows that the code word "pacode" appears in the description of what moved Cyrus to permit the Israelites to return to Jerusalem from their exile in Babylon (Ezra 1:2,3)". Possibly, the Jewish followers of Jesus expected him to use some formulation of "Pacode Yifcode" -God will rendezvous with you, as a sign that he was the Jewish Messiah. By choosing instead the sign of Jonah - a missionary to Nineveh - Jesus implicitly was denying that he was sent to be the Jewish Messiah who would deliver Israel from the yoke of Roman rule.

148 See Luke 11:29, Matthew 12:40; Mark 8:31 and John 2:19.

149 See, e.g., Samuel Lachs, A Rabbinic Commentary on the New Testament: The Gospels of Matthew, Mark and Luke (Ktav Publishing House 1987) at pg. 215.

150 See H. Bialik and Y. Ravnitzky, The Book of Legends - Sefer Ha-Aggadah: Legends From the Talmud and Midrash (Schocken Books 1992) at p. 133 n. 142.

151 See, however, Mark 5:1-20 [Decapolis], Mark 7:24-31 [Tyre, Sidon and Decapolis], Matthew 4:25 [Decapolis] and Matthew 15:21-28 [Tyre and Sidon] where Jesus visited Hellenized centers of Graeco-Roman culture.

152 See M. Ben-Dov, M. Naor and Z. Aner, The Western Wall (Ministry of Defence-Publishing House 1987) at pg. 48.

153 See Robert Backhouse, The Kregel Pictorial Guide to the Temple (Kregel Publications 1996) at pp. 15, 22.

154 See Marvin Wilson, Our Father Abraham: Jewish Roots of the Christian Faith (Wm. Eerdmans Pub. Co. 1989) at pg. 117.

155 See Rabbi H. Donin, To Pray as a Jew (BasicBooks 1980) at pp. 33-37.

156 See S. Wylen, The Jews in the Time of Jesus (Paulist Press 1996) at pg. 91.

157 See R. Moseley, Yeshua: A Guide to the Real Jesus and the Original Church (Lederer Foundation 1996) at pg. 21.

158 See A. Kolatch, This is the Torah (Jonathan David Publishers 1988) at pg. 97.

159 For an extensive discussion of the above points see Dr. R. Moseley, Yeshua: A Guide to the Real Jesus and the Original Church (Lederer Foundation 1996).

160 See Albert Zeitlin, Jesus and the Judaism of His Time (Polity Press 1994) at pp. 65-66.

161 See Talmud, Tractate Berakhot [Blessings] 13b; see Rabbi H. Donin, To Pray as a Jew (BasicBooks 1980) at pp. 144-145.

162 See A. Kolatch, This is the Torah (Jonathan David Publishers 1994) at pp. 234-235.

163 See H. Bialik and Y. Ravnitzky, The Book of Legends -Sefer Ha-Aggadah: Legends From the Talmud and Midrash (Schocken Books 1992) at pg. 9 n. 23.

164 See Avigdor Bonchek, What's Bothering Rashi? A Guide to In- Depth Analysis of his Torah Commentary: Beresheis [Genesis] (Feldheim Publishers 1997) at pg. 13. [Bonchek explains that the conclusion that the light of the first day of creation was set aside in the world to come likely

is based on Psalms 97:11: "The light is sown for the righteous."]

165 See Rabbi M. Munk, The Wisdom in the Hebrew Language (Mesorah Publications 1998) at pg. 100.

166 See The Book of Common Prayer (Oxford University Press 1979) at pg. 864-865.

167 See Rabbi Hillel Fendel, One Thing I Ask: Riddles, Queries and Insights on the Siddur (Feldheim Publishers 1998) at pg. 175- 176; see also, Midrash Tehillim, 27:1: "He wore that Light as if it were a tallit, and from it He 'shined His world'", quoted in Matis Weinberg, FrameWorks: Shemot [Exodus] (Foundation for Jewish Publications 1999) at pg. 226. .

168 See Avigdor Bonchek, What's Bothering Rashi? A Guide to In- Depth Analysis of his Torah Commentary (Beresheis) [Genesis] (Feldheim Publishers 1997) at pg. 22.

169 See Zohar 1:31b, quoted in Matis Weinberg, FrameWorks: Shemot [Exodus] (Foundation for Jewish Publications 1999) at pg. 222.

170 See The Book of Common Prayer (Oxford University Press 1979) at pg. 358.

171 See H. Bialik and Y. Ravnitzky, The Book of Legends -Sefer Ha-Aggadah: Legends From the Talmud and Midrash (Schocken Books 1992) at pg. 9 n. 21.

172 See, Thorleif Boman, Hebrew Thought Compared with Greek Thought (Norton 1970) at pg. 69.

173 See E. Barnavi (ed.), A Historical Atlas of the Jewish People (Schocken Books 1992) at pg. 7.

174 See Talmud, Tractate Tamid (Daily Sacrifice) 17a (2).

175 See, e.g., Rabbi Moshe Weissman, The Midrash Says: Book of Vayikra [Leviticus] (Benei Yakov Publications 1982) at pp. 264- 269.

176 See The Book of Common Prayer (Oxford University Press 1979) at pg. 864).

177 See The Book of Common Prayer (Oxford University Press 1979) at pg. 306).

178 The many and varied attributes and characteristics of the Holy Spirit in the New Testament are fully explored in C. Gunton, The Cambridge Companion to Christian Doctrine (Cambridge University Press 1997) at pp. 273-296.

179 See Geza Vermes, Jesus the Jew (Fortress Press 1981) at pp. 24-25.

180 See Rabbi M. Weissman, The Midrash Says: The Book of Vayikra [Leviticus] (Benei Yakov Publications 1997) at pg. 120.

181 See, e.g., Deuteronomy 24:8-9, where it is noted that leprosy was visited by God upon Miriam for speaking evil of Moses.

182 See Rabbi M. Weissman, The Midrash Says: The Book of Vayikra [Leviticus] (Benei Yakov Publications 1997) at pp. 121-132.

183 See Weissman, ibid. at pg. 133.

184 See Weissman, ibid. at pg. 121.

185 See Weissman, ibid. at pg. 136.

186 See Rabbi Moshe Weissman, <u>The Midrash Says: The Book of Beraishis [Genesis]</u> (Bnei Yakov Publications 1999) at pg. 173.

187 See A. Kolatch, <u>This is the Torah</u> (Jonathan David Publishers 1994) at pg. 44.

188 See Rabbi Adin Steinsaltz, <u>The Talmud: A Reference Guide</u> (Random House 1989) at pg. 251.

189 See, Rabbi Nosson Scherman, <u>The Kaddish Prayer</u> (Mesorah Publications, Ltd. 1997) at pp. vii, 26-27 and 49.

190 See Rabbi H. Donin, <u>To Pray as a Jew</u> (BasicBooks 1980) at p. 216).

191 See Rabbi H. Donin, <u>To Pray as a Jew</u> (BasicBooks 1980) at pg. 213.

192 See Rabbi Hillel Fendel, <u>One Thing I Ask: Riddles, Queries and Insights on the Siddur</u> (Feldheim Publishers 1998) at pg. 39.

193 Quoted in Geza Vermes, <u>The Religion of Jesus the Jew</u> (Fortress Press 1993) at pg. 132.

194 All quotes from the Didache are from K. Lake (translator), <u>The Apostolic Fathers: Volume 1</u> (Harvard University Press: Loeb Classical Library 1998) beginning at pg. 305.

195 See Kurt Niederwimmer, <u>The Didache</u> (Augsburg Fortress 1998).

196 See Kurt Niederwimmer, <u>The Didache</u> (Augsburg Fortress 1998) at pg. 127.

197 See Kurt Niederwimmer, <u>The Didache</u> (Augsburg Fortress 1998) at pp. 144-147.

198 See Kurt Niederwimmer, <u>The Didache</u> (Augsburg Fortress 1998) at pg. 151.

199 See Kurt Niederwimmer, <u>The Didache</u> (Augsburg Fortress 1998) at pg. 155.

200 See Kurt Niederwimmer, <u>The Didache</u> (Augsburg Fortress 1998) at pp. 191-193.

201 Quoted in Geza Vermes, <u>The Religion of Jesus the Jew</u> (Fortress Books 1993) at pg. 202.

202 See Rabbi M. Weissman, <u>The Midrash Says: The Book of Vayikra [Leviticus]</u> (Benei Yakov Publications 1997) at pg. 87.

203 See Rabbi Adin Steinsaltz, <u>The Talmud: A Reference Guide</u> (Random House 1989) at pg. 164.

204 See Talmud, Tractate Yoma (Day of Atonement) 75a.

205 See Matis Weinberg, <u>FrameWorks: Bereishit [Genesis]</u> (Foundation for Jewish Publications 1999) at pg. 308; see also Rabbi Adin Steinsaltz, <u>The Talmud: A Reference Guide</u> (Random House 1989) at pg. 242; see Joshua 21:8-19.

206 See Talmud, Tractate Yoma (Day of Atonement) 73a.

207 See, e.g., Geza Vermes, <u>The Religion of Jesus the Jew</u> (Fortress Press 1993) at pp. 5-6, 146-148, 210-215.

208 See Schlesinger and Vogel, <u>The Ten Commandments</u> (HarperCollins 1998) at pg. 98.

209 See W. Harter, "The Christian Search for Jewish Roots", <u>Keeping Posted</u>, Vol. XIX, No. 3 (UAHC Dec. 1973).

210 See Peter Stravinskas, <u>The Catholic Church and the Bible</u> (Ignatius Press 1987) at pg. 58.

211 See, James Strong, <u>The Tabernacle of Israel</u> (Kregel Publications 1987) at pg. 65 n. 62: "Wine was poured out as a libation (heb. nesek, a pouring...) in connection with many sacrifices

on the great Altar").

212 See, e.g., Rabbi M. Weissman, The Midrash Says: The Book of Vayikra [Leviticus] (Benei Yakov Publications 1997) at pg. 58; see also Leviticus 7:26-27.

213 See H. Attridge, "Christianity from the Destruction of Jerusalem to Constantine's Adoption of the New Religion: 70-312 C.E.", in Hershel Shanks (ed.), Christianity and Rabbinic Judaism: A Parallel History of Their Origins and Early Development (Biblical Archaeology Society 1992) at pg. 157.

214 See entry under "Temple" in the Encyclopedia Judaica (Judaica Multimedia/Keter Publishing House: CD ROM Edition): "nor could the sacrifice of an individual be offered if he was not present."

215 See Rabbi Adin Steinsaltz, The Talmud: A Reference Guide (Random House 1989) at pg. 251.

216 See Rabbi M. Weissman, The Midrash: The Book of Vayikra [Leviticus] (Bnai Yaakov 1997) at pp. 19-24.

217 See Rabbi M. Weissman, The Midrash: The Book of Vayikra [Leviticus] (Bnai Yaakov 1997) at pp. 19-24, 57.

218 Rabbi Ira Stone, Seeking the Path to Life: Theological Mediations on God and the Nature of People, Love, Life and Death (Jewish Lights Publishing 1992) at pg. 32. Indeed, only through familiarity with Second Temple sacrificial rituals can one fully understand the structure of the modern-day Synagogue services. As examples of this influence, it has been noted in Stephen Schach, The Structure of the Siddur (Jason Aronson, Inc. 1996) that: (a) the Amidah prayer in the Additional Service includes a blessing relating to God's institution of the Sabbath Temple offerings in a progression of blessings from creation to revelation, to Temple sacrificial offerings to redemption (pg. 30), (b) the third section of the traditional Sabbath Amidah gives thanks for God's mercy, petitions for peace and petitions for the restoration of the Temple service (see page 34), (c) on the Sabbath Additional Service for Rosh Chodesh (New Month Festival), the fourth blessing of the Amidah lists the Second Temple sacrificial offerings (Numbers 28:9-10) (see page 41), (d) during the weekday services on Rosh Chodesh and Chol haMo-ed (Intermediate Days of Pesach and Sukkot), but not on festivals such as Purim and Chanukah which were added after the destruction of the Second Temple by the Rabbis, the seventeenth blessing of the Amidah has added to it the prayer "Eloheinu Velohei avoteinu, ya'aleh v'yavo" (Our God and God of our fathers, [may the remembrance] ascend and come), which evokes the Temple sacrifices (see pp. 61-62), (e) there is no Priestly Blessing [Birkat Kohanim] in the weekday Amidah for the Evening Service, because the Priests in the Second Temple blessed the people during the Morning Service and the Additional Service only (see page 64), (f) a central part of the Additional Service (Musaf) Amidah is a description of the relevant sacrificial offerings which were offered in the Second Temple on that day (e.g., Sabbath/festival day: Numbers 28:9-10; Pesach: Numbers 28:16-19 and Numbers 28:19; Shavuot: Numbers 28:26-27; Sukkot: Numbers

29:12-36), together with a reference to the meal and libation offerings after each specific Festival passage (Numbers 28:12-15) (see pages 73-74), (g) Psalm 100 is not said in modern-day Synagogues on Shabbat, on erev Yom Kippur (eve of Yom Kippur) or on erev Pesach because Psalm 100 was recited in the Second Temple when individual thank offerings were sacrificed and on Shabbat, erev Yom Kippur and erev Pesach only communal offerings were sacrificed at the Second Temple (see page 160), (h) during the Festival Sabbath Morning Service, the Maftir (additional or completion) readings from the Torah are from Numbers 25:10-29;40) describing the Temple sacrifices for the relevant festival (see page 184), (i) before returning the Torah scroll to the Ark during Festival services in anticipation of reciting the Ashrei prayer, the prayer "Yah Eli" (O Lord, my God) is recited, which recalls the Temple services and expresses the hope that some day the worshippers may be able to recite the Ashrei prayer in the rebuilt Temple (see page 196), (j) the Preliminary Morning Service contains Korbanot (sacrifice) prayers and excerpts from the Torah which describe the laver the Priests used to pour on their hands and feet, the removal of the ashes from the altar, the daily (Tamid) offering, the incense, all in the belief that "forgiveness from sin can be achieved by recitation of the order of sacrifices and that this activity is equivalent to offering the sacrifices themselves" (see page 230), and (k) the introduction of the Musaf (Additional) Service in Synagogues was to take the place of the Musaf sacrifice which was offered in the Second Temple on Shabbat, Festivals, Chol haMo-ed and Rosh Chodesh, with the fourth blessing of the Amidah being devoted to the Temple and its sacrificial offerings (see page 237).

219 See, e.g., S. Wylen, The Jews in the Time of Jesus (Paulist Press 1996) at pp. 89-90.

220 See Talmud, Tractate Yoma (Day of Atonement) 85b.

221 See F. Ferguson, A Pilgrimage of Faith: An Introduction to the Episcopal Church (Morehouse-Barlow Co. 1957) at pg. 11.

222 See Talmud, Tractate Tamid (Daily Sacrifice) 29b (11): "Like all holy things, it was immersed in water before being used."

223 See Rabbi Adin Steinsaltz, The Talmud: A Reference Guide (Random House 1989) at pg. 177.

224 See H. Bialik and Y. Ravnitzky, The Book of Legends - Sefer Ha-Aggadah: Legends From the Talmud and Midrash (Schocken Books 1992) at p.350 n. 128.

225 See Rabbi M. Weissman, The Midrash Says: The Book of Vayikra [Leviticus] (Benei Yaakov Publications 1982) at pg. 60.

226 See Talmud, Tractate Berakhot (Blessings) 57b: "Five things contain a sixtieth part of five other things: fire is a sixtieth of hell, honey a sixtieth of manna, the Sabbath a sixtieth of the rest of the World to Come, sleep a sixtieth of death, and a dream, a sixtieth of prophesy."

227 See Philip Yancey, The Bible Jesus Read (Zondervan Publishing House 1999) at pg. 70.

228 See Robert Alter, The Art of Biblical Poetry (BasicBooks 1985) at pp. 103-104, 110.

229 See Avigdor Bonchek, What's Bothering Rashi: A Guide to In- Depth Analysis of his Torah

Commentary: The Book of Shemos [Exodus] (Feldheim Publishers 1999) at pp. 29-31.

230 See Talmud, Tractate Nedarim (Vows) 64b.

231 Gaon Rabbeinu Eliyahu.

232 See Geza Vermes, Jesus the Jew: A Historian's Reading of the Gospels (Fortress Press 1973) at pg. 83 et seq.

233 See Irving Zeitlin, Jesus and the Judaism of His Time (Polity Press 1994) at pp. 142-143; see also Wise/Abbeg/Cook at pg. 33; William Klassen, Judas: Betrayer or Friend of Jesus? (Fortress Press 1996) at pg. 32.

234 See Zeitlin, ibid. at pp. 143.

235 See William Klassen, Judas: Betrayer or Friend of Jesus? (Fortress Press 1996) at pg. 150: "How radically the act of Jesus violated contemporary standards has been documented by Duncan Derrett. He reminds us that the washing of feet was reserved for slaves; in the Hebrew tradition Abraham delicately suggested that his heavenly visitors could wash their own feet (Gen 18:4). Even the high priest washed his own feet on the Day of Atonement."

236 See William Klassen, Judas: Betrayer or Friend of Jesus? (Fortress Press 1996) at pg. 98.

237 See, e.g., Daniel 12:1-2; see also S. Wylen, The Jews in the Time of Jesus (Paulist Press 1996) at pg. 59-61.

238 See The Book of Common Prayer (Oxford University Press 1979) at pg. 15.

239 See Rabbi A. Feuer and S. Finkelman (compilers), Tishah B'Av -Texts, Readings and Insights (Mesorah Publications Ltd. 1997) at pg. 62.

240 See Rabbi Moshe Weissman, What the Midrash Says: The Book of Beraishis [Genesis] (Bnai Yakov Publications 1999) at pg. 14.

241 See (A. Kolatch, This is the Torah (Jonathan David Publishers 1998) at pg. 33.

242 See, e.g., "The Gifts and the Calling of God are Irrevocable (Rom 11:29): A Reflection on Theological Questions Pertaining to Catholic-Jewish Relations on the 50th Anniversary of 'Nostra Aetate' (No. 4)", December 10, 2015, at http://www.vatican.va/roman_curia/ pontifical_councils/chrstuni/sub-index/index_relations-jews.htm

243 See Siddur Sim Shalom (The Rabbinical Assembly 1985) at pg. 635.

244 See Robert Funk, Roy Hoover and the Jesus Seminar, The Five Gospels (HarperSanFrancisco 1997) at pg. 2.

245 See Robert Funk and the Jesus Seminar, The Acts of Jesus: What Did Jesus Really Do? (HarperSanFrancisco 1999) at pg. 1.

246 See M. Wilkins and J. P. Moreland (ed.), Jesus Under Fire (Zondervan Publishing House 1995).

247 The debate was recounted in Paul Copan (ed.), Will the Real Jesus Please Stand Up? (Baker Books 1998).

248 See Copan, ibid., at pg. 39.

249 See Copan, ibid. at pg. 51.

250 See, e.g., Stanley J. Grenz, <u>A Primer on Postmodernism</u> (William B. Eerdmans Publishing Co. 1996) at pp. 44-45.

251 See "http://www.shj.org".

252 See "http://www.csjo.org/".

253 See C. Gunton (ed.), <u>The Cambridge Companion to Christian Doctrine</u> (Cambridge University Press 1997) at pg. 293.

254 See Avigdor Bonchek, <u>What's Bothering Rashi? A Guide to the In-Depth Analysis of his Torah Commentary: Shemos [Exodus]</u> (Feldheim Publishers 1999) at pg. 32.

255 See Dr. Laura Schlesinger and Rabbi Stewart Vogel, <u>The Ten Commandments</u> (HarperCollins 1998) at pg. 33.

256 See Matis Weinberg, <u>FrameWorks: Bereishit [Genesis]</u> (Foundation for Jewish Publications 1999) at pg. 76.

257 See Rabbi Carol Harris-Shapiro, <u>Messianic Judaism</u> (Beacon Press 1999) at pp. 172-173 and 187.

258 See, e.g., Rabbi Hayim Donin, <u>To Pray as a Jew</u> (BasicBooks 1980) at pp. 200-201.

259 See Marvin Wilson, <u>Our Father Abraham: Jewish Roots of the Christian Faith</u> (William B. Eerdmans Co. 1989) at pp. xvi, 4.

260 See Midrash Hagadol, Bereishit 25:31, quoted in Matis Weinberg, <u>FrameWorks: Bereishit [Genesis]</u> (Foundation for Jewish Publications 1999) at pg. 189.

261 See, e.g., John Leith (ed.), <u>Creeds of the Churches</u> (John Knox Press 1982).

262 The evolving concepts of the resurrection of the body in Judaism from earliest Biblical times to later rabbinic periods is thoroughly discussed in Neil Gillman, <u>The Death of Death: Resurrection and Immortality in Jewish Thought</u> (Jewish Lights Publishing 1997).

263 See, e.g., "What is Reform?", <u>Keeping Posted</u>, Vol. XXIV, No. 1 (UAHC Sept. 1978); "Orthodox Judaism", <u>Keeping Posted,</u> Vol. XXV, No. 4 (UAHC Jan. 1980); "Conservative Judaism", <u>Keeping Posted</u>, Vol. XXVI, No. 3 (UAHC Dec. 1980); see also, Rabbi Yechiel Eckstein, <u>How Firm a Foundation: A Gift of Jewish Wisdom for Christians and Jews</u> (Paraclete Press 1997) at pp. 219-241.

264 See, e.g., Jaroslav Pelikan, <u>Jesus Through the Centuries</u> (Harper and Row 1985) at pg. 19.

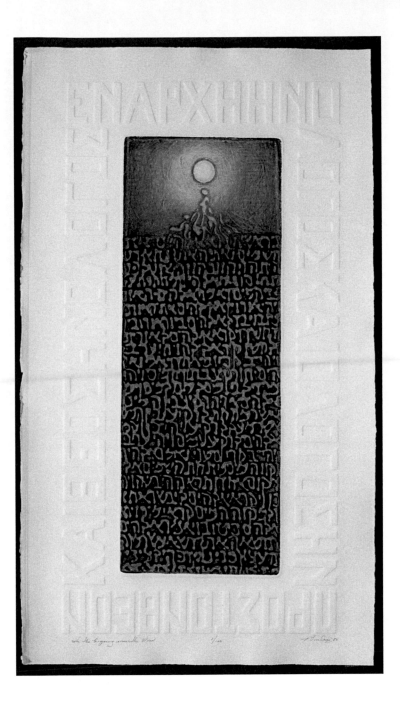

"In the Beginning Was the Word"

This piece portrays an exchange between the Old and New Testaments. The Hebrew text, "In the beginning God created," begins the first chapter of Genesis and is the central focus of this print. A Greek embossing surrounds the Hebrew with "In the beginning was the Word...the Word became flesh and dwelt among us." John 1:1 & 13. Collagraph and embossing 1982 30" x 18" - Sandra Bowden